About This Book

The JIST enhanced version of *Federal Benefits for Veterans and Dependents*, 2000 Edition, includes the full text of the original Department of Veterans Affairs publication, plus informative bonus sections about the Federal government's hiring preferences for veterans and reference materials for locating VA forms, facts, and answers online.

A new feature in this year's edition of the Federal Benefits handbook is an icon added to indicate information that may change during the year, due to legislative or other actions. You'll see this icon ◼ and explanation found on page 11. You should be alerted to doublecheck any information that appears with this icon to ensure that it's current.

About Your Domain Publishing

Your Domain Publishing, an imprint of JIST Publishing, Inc., is committed to producing value-added government resources and providing greater access to the wealth of public domain information that is available. A portion of the net profits from Your Domain books is donated to charity.

We hope you find this high-quality reprint a handy resource and the bonus sections especially useful. Please feel free to contact us at editorial@jist.com with any comments or questions.

**Department of
Veterans Affairs**

2000 Edition

Federal Benefits for

Veterans

and Dependents

Contents

Introduction

This pamphlet lists the variety of federal benefits available to veterans and their dependents. Eligibility depends upon individual circumstances. Contact the nearest VA benefits office at 1-800-827-1000 from any location in the United States to apply. Counselors can answer questions about benefits eligibility and application procedures. They also make referrals to other VA facilities, such as medical centers and national cemeteries. Phone numbers of VA offices, including those in the Philippines and Puerto Rico, are listed in the back of this book. VA facilities also are listed in the federal government section of telephone directories under Department of Veterans Affairs.

Health-care Enrollment. For most veterans, entry into the VA health-care system starts with enrollment at a VA health-care facility. Once enrolled, a veteran is eligible to receive services without further processing. Details of the enrollment program are discussed in the Health-Care Benefits section of this publication. VA health-care facilities also provide information on medical care, including readjustment counseling, and examinations for Agent Orange, radiation exposure and ailments incurred from service in the Gulf War.

Who's Eligible. Eligibility for most VA benefits is based upon discharge from active military service under other than dishonorable conditions. Active service means full-time service as a member of the Army, Navy, Air Force, Marines, Coast Guard, or as a commissioned officer of the Public Health Service, the Environmental Services Administration or the National Oceanic and Atmospheric Administration. Completion of at least six years of honorable service in the Selected Reserves also provides home-loan benefits for those not otherwise eligible. Persons serving in the reserves also can receive education benefits. Men and women veterans with similar service are entitled to the same VA benefits. Service in 30 organizations during special periods that include World Wars I and II has been certified as active military service by the Defense Department. Members of these groups, listed on pages 54 - 56, may be eligible for

9

VA benefits if the Defense Department certifies their service and issues a discharge under other than dishonorable conditions.

Honorable and general discharges qualify a veteran for most VA benefits. Dishonorable and bad conduct discharges issued by general courts-martial bar VA benefits. Veterans in prison and parolees may be eligible for certain VA benefits. VA regional offices can clarify eligibility of prisoners and parolees.

Wartime Service. Certain VA benefits and medical care require wartime service. Under the law, VA recognizes these war periods:

Mexican Border Period — May 9, 1916, through April 5, 1917, for veterans who served in Mexico, on its borders or in adjacent waters.

World War I — April 6, 1917, through Nov. 11, 1918; for veterans who served in Russia, April 6, 1917, through April 1, 1920; extended through July 1, 1921, for veterans who had at least one day of service between April 6, 1917, and Nov. 11, 1918.

World War II — Dec. 7, 1941, through Dec. 31, 1946.

Korean Conflict — June 27, 1950, through Jan. 31, 1955.

Vietnam Era — Aug. 5, 1964 (Feb. 28, 1961, for veterans who served "in country" before Aug. 5, 1964), through May 7, 1975.

Gulf War — Aug. 2, 1990, through a date to be set by law or Presidential Proclamation.

Filing Claims. Those seeking a VA benefit for the first time must submit a copy of their service discharge, DD-214, which documents service dates and type of discharge, or give their full name, military service number, branch of service and dates of service. The claim number assigned by VA to the initial claim should be referred to in subsequent correspondence.

Important Documents. The veteran's DD-214 form should be kept in a safe location accessible to the veteran and next of kin or designated representative. The veteran's preference regarding burial in a national cemetery and use of a headstone provided by VA should be documented and kept with this information. The following documents will be needed for claims processing related to a veteran's death: (1) veteran's marriage certificate for claims of a surviving spouse or children; (2) veteran's death certificate if the veteran did not die in a VA health-care facility; (3) children's birth certificates to determine children's benefits; (4) veteran's birth certificate to determine parents' benefits.

This pamphlet contains information on benefits and programs that is accurate as of January 1, 2000. Changes may occur during the year as a result of legislative or other requirements. Those areas in which changes are most likely to occur are indicated with the following symbol: ■ . Call your nearest benefits or health-care facility to obtain the latest information on these topics.

Información Para Veteranos De Habla Hispana y Sus Dependientes

La versión en español de este folleto se encuentra disponible en formato Adobe Acrobat a través de el link http://www.va.gov/opa/feature/index.htm en la página de la Oficina de Asuntos Públicos del Departamento de Asuntos de Veteranos (VA) en la red mundial del internet. Las oficinas del VA en areas de gran concentración de veteranos y dependientes hispanos tienen disponibles consejeros bilingües que le pueden ayudar a aplicar para obtener beneficios. Puede encotrar una lista de las oficinas del VA en la parte de atrás de este folleto.

11

HEALTH-CARE BENEFITS

Health-Care Enrollment

To receive health care, veterans generally must be enrolled with VA. A veteran may apply for enrollment at any time. Veterans do not have to be enrolled if they: (1) have a service-connected disability of 50 percent or more; (2) want care for a disability, which the military determined was incurred or aggravated in the line of duty, but which VA has not yet rated, during the 12-month period following discharge; or (3) want care for a service-connected disability. To permit better planning of health resources, however, these three categories of veterans also are urged to enroll.

Veterans will be enrolled to the extent Congressional appropriations allow. If appropriations are limited, enrollment will occur based on the following priorities:

1. Veterans with service-connected conditions who are rated 50 percent or more disabled.

2. Veterans with service-connected conditions who are rated 30 or 40 percent disabled.

3. Veterans who are former POWs or were awarded a Purple Heart, veterans with disabilities rated 10 and 20 percent, and veterans awarded special eligibility for disabilities incurred in treatment.

4. Veterans who are receiving aid and attendance or housebound benefits and veterans who have been determined by VA to be catastrophically disabled.

5. Nonservice-connected veterans and service-connected veterans rated zero percent, noncompensable disabled, who are determined to be unable to defray the expenses of needed care.

6. All other eligible veterans who are not required to make copayments for their treatment. This includes veterans of the Mexican border period or of World War I; veterans solely seeking care for a disorder associated with exposure to a toxic substance or radiation, for a disorder associated with service in the Southwest Asia theater of operations during the Gulf War, or for any illness associated with service in combat in a war after the Gulf War or during a period of hostility after November 11, 1998, as provided and limited in 38 U.S.C. 1710(e); and veterans with 0 percent service-

connected disabilities who are nevertheless compensated, including veterans receiving compensation for inactive tuberculosis.

7. Nonservice-connected veterans and noncompensable zero percent service-connected veterans who agree to pay copayments.

These groups are enrollment priorities only. The services and treatment available to enrolled veterans is not based on enrollment priority groups. Enrollment will be reviewed each year and veterans will be notified in writing of any change in their enrollment status. Additional information on enrollment, including enrollment forms and on-line applications, can be found on the World Wide Web (http://www.va.gov/health/elig/).

The Veterans' Millennium Health Care and Benefits Act of 1999 authorized VA to expand long-term care services and to reimburse emergency treatment expenses for certain enrolled veterans. It also authorized VA to place Purple Heart recipients into Priority Group Three unless they are otherwise eligible for a higher Priority Group. This legislation may result in additional changes to health-care benefits during the year. Call your nearest health-care facility or the Health Benefits Service Center, 1-877-222-8387, to obtain the latest information. ◨

Financial Assessment

Veterans who want to enroll in priority group 5 based on their inability to defray the cost of their care must provide VA with information on their annual income and net worth to determine whether they are below the "means test" threshold; or agree to copayment requirements. The threshold is adjusted annually and announced in January. In making the assessment, the veteran's household income is considered.

The "means test" eligibility assessment includes Social Security, U.S. Civil Service retirement, U.S. Railroad Retirement, military retirement, unemployment insurance, any other retirement income, total wages from all employers, interest and dividends, workers' compensation, black lung benefits and any other gross income for the calendar year prior to application for care. Also considered are assets such as the market value of stocks, bonds, notes, individual retirement accounts, bank deposits, savings accounts and cash. The patient may fill out VA Form 10-10EZ at the time application for enrollment is made. VA forms can be found on the World Wide Web at the VA forms website (http://www.va.gov/forms/default.asp).

VA may compare income information provided by the veteran with information obtained from the Social Security Administration and the Internal Revenue Service.

Copayments

After a veteran completes a financial assessment that determines the veteran's income is above the "means test" threshold, the veteran *must* agree to pay copayments to be eligible for VA care. If a veteran does not agree to make the copayments the veteran will be ineligible for VA care. VA holds these patients whose income is determined to be above the "means test" threshold responsible for the Medicare deductible for the first 90 days of care during any 365-day period. For each additional 90 days of hospital care, the patient is charged one-half the Medicare deductible. For each additional 90 days of nursing-home care, the patient is again charged the full Medicare deductible. In addition to these charges, the patient is charged $10 a day for hospital care and $5 a day for VA nursing-home care. For outpatient care, the copayment is 20 percent of the cost of an average outpatient visit.

Billing Insurance Companies

When applying for medical care, all veterans will be asked to provide information pertaining to health insurance coverage, including policies held by spouses. VA is authorized to submit claims to insurance carriers for the recovery of costs for medical care provided to nonservice-connected veterans and service-connected veterans for nonservice-connected conditions. Veterans will not be responsible for portions of an insurance claim not covered by the policy. Veterans above certain income levels, however, are responsible for the copayments required by federal law.

Nursing-Home Care

Nursing care in VA or private nursing homes may be provided for veterans who are not acutely ill and not in need of hospital care. VA will provide needed nursing-home care to any veteran in need of such care for a service-connected disability, and to any veteran who needs such care and who has a service-connected disability rated at 70 percent or more. This authority will expire on December 31, 2003. In addition, if space and resources are available, VA may also provide VA nursing-home care to other veterans. Veterans who have a service-connected disability are given first priority for nursing-home care. Applicants who may be provided nursing-home care without an income eligibility assessment include veterans with a compensable, service-connected disability, veterans who were exposed to herbicides while serving in Vietnam, veterans exposed to ionizing radiation during atmospheric testing or in the occupation of Hiroshima and Nagasaki, veterans with a condition related to an environmental exposure in the Gulf War, veterans who are former prisoners of war, veterans on VA pension, veterans of the Mexican Border period or World War I and veterans who are eligible for Medicaid.

Nonservice-connected veterans and zero percent, noncompensable, service-connected veterans requiring nursing-home care for any nonservice-connected disability must complete the financial section on VA Form 10-10EZ, to determine whether they will be billed for nursing-home care. Income assessment procedures are the same as for hospital care.

Veterans who are receiving health care from VA may be transferred to a private nursing home at VA expense. VA-authorized care normally may not be provided in excess of six months, except for veterans who need nursing-home care for a service-connected disability or veterans who were hospitalized primarily for treatment of a service-connected disability.

Direct admission to private nursing homes at VA expense is limited to: (1) a veteran who requires nursing care for a service-connected disability after medical determination by VA; (2) a patient in a military hospital who requires a protracted period of nursing care and who will become a veteran upon discharge from the Armed Forces; and (3) a veteran who had been discharged from a VA medical center and is receiving home health services from VA. Portions of the nursing-home care program may vary from what is indicated here as a result of recent legislation. Call your nearest benefits or health-care facility to obtain the latest information. ◘

Domiciliary Care

Domiciliary care provides rehabilitative and long-term, health-maintenance care for veterans who require minimal medical care but who do not need the skilled nursing services provided in nursing homes. VA may provide domiciliary care to veterans whose annual income does not exceed the maximum annual rate of VA pension or to veterans the Secretary of Veterans Affairs determines have no adequate means of support. This program may vary from what is indicated here as a result of recent legislation. Call your nearest benefits or health-care facility to obtain the latest information. ◻

Outpatient Pharmacy Services

Outpatient pharmacy services are provided free to: (1) veterans with a service-connected disability of 50 percent or more; (2) veterans receiving medication for treatment of service-connected conditions; (3) veterans whose income does not exceed the maximum VA pension. Other veterans will be charged $2 for each 30-day or less supply of medication. As a result of recent legislation, the copayment amount may change, and VA may implement maximum monthly and maximum annual copayment amounts for veterans with multiple outpatient prescriptions.

Outpatient Dental Treatment

Outpatient dental treatment provided by VA includes examinations and the full spectrum of diagnostic, surgical, restorative and preventive procedures. Some veterans receiving dental care may be billed the applicable copayment if their income exceeds the maximum threshold. The following veterans may receive care: (1) veterans having service-connected and compensable dental disabilities or conditions; (2) former prisoners of war incarcerated 90 days or more; (3) veterans with service-connected, noncompensable dental conditions as a result of combat wounds or service injuries; (4) veterans with nonservice-connected dental conditions determined by VA to be aggravating a medical problem; (5) veterans having service-connected conditions rated at 100 percent; and (6) veterans participating in a vocational rehabilitation program. Veterans may receive one-time dental treatment for service-connected and noncompensable dental disabilities or conditions if the following conditions are met: the dental condition can be shown to have existed at time of discharge; the veteran served on active military duty for at least 180 days, (or 90 days during Gulf War Era); the veteran applied to VA for dental care within 90 days of discharge or release from active duty, and the certificate of discharge does not include certification that all appropriate dental treatment had been rendered prior to discharge.

Gulf War, Agent Orange and Ionizing Radiation

Registry Programs. Veterans who served in the Gulf War (August 2, 1990 to a date not yet established) or who claim exposure to Agent Orange during the Vietnam War (between 1962 and 1975), or atomic radiation, or veterans treated with Nasopharyngeal (NP) radium during military service, are provided with free, comprehensive

16

medical examinations, including laboratory and other diagnostic tests deemed necessary by an examining physician to determine health status. Eligible veterans do not have to be enrolled in VA health care to participate in registry examinations. Results of the examinations, which include review of the veteran's military service and exposure history, are entered into special, computerized databases, called registries. These databases assist VA in analyzing the types of health conditions being reported by veterans. Registry participants are advised of the results of their examinations in personal consultations and by letters. Veterans wishing to participate should contact the nearest VA health-care facility for an examination.

VA operates a toll-free hotline at 800-749-8387 to inform Gulf War veterans about VA programs, their benefits and the latest information on Gulf War Era benefits.

Treatment. VA provides treatment to any Gulf War veteran who has a medical condition that may be the result of Gulf War service. A veteran who, while serving in Vietnam, may have been exposed to dioxin or to a toxic substance in a herbicide or defoliant used for military purposes, is provided medical treatment by VA for conditions possibly related to such exposure. Health-care services also are available for medical conditions the VA recognizes as possibly related to a veteran's exposure to ionizing radiation from the detonation of a nuclear device in connection with nuclear tests (between 1945 and 1962), or with the American occupation of Hiroshima and Nagasaki, Japan, during the period beginning Sept. 11, 1945, and ending July 1, 1946; or internment as a prisoner of war in Japan during World War II which VA determines resulted in exposure to ionizing radiation, or treatment of any cancer of the head or neck which VA finds may be associated with the veteran's receipt of NP radium irradiation treatments while in the active military.

Beneficiary Travel
Veterans may be eligible for payment or reimbursement for travel costs to receive VA medical care. Travel payments are subject to a deductible of $3 for each one-way trip and an $18-per-month maximum payment. Two exceptions to the deductible are travel for a compensation or pension examination and travel by special modes of transportation, such as an ambulance or a specially equipped van. Beneficiary travel payments may be made to the following: (1) veterans whose service-connected disabilities are rated at 30 percent

or more; (2) veterans traveling for treatment of a service-connected condition; (3) veterans who receive a VA pension; (4) veterans traveling for scheduled compensation or pension examinations; (5) veterans whose income does not exceed the maximum VA pension rate; and (6) veterans whose medical condition requires use of a special mode of transportation, if the veteran is unable to defray the costs and travel is pre-authorized. If the medical condition is a medical emergency, travel need not be pre-authorized when a delay would be hazardous.

Alcohol- and Drug-Dependence Treatment

Veterans eligible for VA medical care may apply for substance abuse treatment. Contact the nearest VA medical facility to enroll for care.

Home Improvements and Structural Alterations

The Home Improvements and Structural Alterations program provides funding for eligible veterans to make home improvements necessary for the continuation of treatment or for disability access to the home and essential lavatory and sanitary facilities. Home improvement benefits up to $4,100 for service-connected veterans and up to $1,200 for nonservice-connected veterans may be provided. For application information, contact the prosthetic representative at the nearest VA medical center or outpatient clinic.

Prosthetic and Sensory Aid Services

VA provides medically prescribed prosthetic and sensory aids to eligible veterans. These aids include artificial limbs, hearing aids, communication aids, eyeglasses, orthopedic braces and shoes, wheelchairs, crutches and canes. For additional information, contact the prosthetic representative at the nearest VA medical center or outpatient clinic.

Services and Aids for Blind Veterans

Blind veterans may be eligible for services at a VA medical center or for admission to a VA blind rehabilitation center. Services are available at all VA medical facilities through the Visual Impairment Services coordinator. In addition, blind veterans entitled to receive disability compensation may receive VA aids for the blind.
Aids and services for blind veterans include:
    1. A total health and benefits review by a VA Visual Impairment Services team.
    2. Adjustment to blindness training.

3.   Home improvements and structural alterations to homes.
4.   Specially adapted housing and adaptations.
5.   Low-vision aids and training in their use.
6.   Electronic and mechanical aids for the blind, including adaptive computers and computer-assisted devices such as reading machines and electronic travel aids.
7.   Guide dogs, including the expense of training the veteran to use the dog and the cost of the dog's medical care.
8.   Talking books, tapes and Braille literature.

Readjustment Counseling

Readjustment counseling is provided at Vet Centers to help veterans resolve psychological war trauma and to help them achieve a successful post-war adjustment to civilian life. Assistance includes group, individual and family counseling. Eligible for counseling are veterans who served on active duty in a combat theater during World War II, the Korean Conflict, the Vietnam Era, the Gulf War, or the campaigns in Lebanon, Grenada, Panama or Somalia. Veterans who served in the active military during the Vietnam Era are also eligible, provided they have requested services at a Vet Center before January 1, 2004.

Psychological readjustment problems include post traumatic stress disorder, or PTSD. This refers to such symptoms as nightmares, intrusive recollections or memories, anxiety or sudden reactions following exposure to traumatic wartime conditions. Readjustment difficulties may affect functioning in school, family or work. Counseling also is provided for trauma due to sexual assault or harassment while on active duty. In areas distant from Vet Centers or VA medical facilities, veterans may obtain readjustment counseling from private-sector professionals who are on contract with VA. To obtain additional information about available services, contact the nearest Vet Center.

Special Categories for Medical Care

Merchant Marine Seamen

Merchant Marine seamen who served in World War II may qualify for veterans benefits. When applying for medical care, seamen must present their DD-214 discharge certificate from the Defense Department to the VA medical facility. VA regional offices can assist in obtaining a certificate.

Allied Veterans

VA is authorized to provide medical care to veterans of nations allied or associated with the United States during World War I or World War II. Such treatment is available at any VA medical facility if authorized and reimbursed by the foreign government. VA also is authorized to provide hospitalization, outpatient and domiciliary care to former members of the armed forces of Czechoslovakia or Poland who participated during World Wars I or II in armed conflict against an enemy of the United States, if they have been citizens of the United States for at least 10 years.

Medical Care for Dependents and Survivors

CHAMPVA, the VA Civilian Health and Medical Program, shares the cost of medical care for dependents and survivors of veterans. If not eligible for TRICARE (the medical program for civilian dependents provided by the Defense Department) or Medicare, Part A, as a result of reaching age 65, the following are eligible for CHAMPVA:

1. The spouse or child of a veteran who has a permanent and total service-connected disability.
2. The spouse or child of a veteran who died of a service-connected condition or was totally disabled from a service-connected condition at the time of death.
3. The spouse or child of a person who died in the line of duty, and not due to misconduct.

A widow or widower who lost eligibility for medical care under CHAMPVA as a result of remarriage may regain eligibility upon termination of the remarriage.

Persons under age 65 must be enrolled in both Medicare Parts A and B to be eligible for CHAMPVA as a secondary payer to Medicare. Beneficiaries age 65 or older who lose eligibility for CHAMPVA by becoming eligible for Medicare, Part A, may re-establish CHAMPVA eligibility by submitting documentation from the Social Security Administration certifying they are not entitled to or have exhausted Medicare, Part A, benefits. Apply to the VA Health Administration Center, P.O. Box 65023, Denver, CO 80206, or call 1-800-733-8387. Additional information on CHAMPVA benefits, eligibility, and application procedures and forms is available on the World Wide Web (www.va.gov/hac/champva/champva.html).

BENEFIT PROGRAMS FOR VETERANS

Disability Compensation

Monetary benefits, called disability compensation, are paid to veterans who are disabled by injury or disease incurred or aggravated during active military service. The service of the veteran must have been terminated through separation or discharge under conditions that were other than dishonorable. Disability compensation varies with the degree of disability and the number of dependents, and is paid monthly. The benefits are not subject to federal or state income tax. The payment of military retirement pay, disability severance pay and separation incentive payments known as SSB and VSI (Special Separation Benefits and Voluntary Separation Incentives) also affects the amount of VA compensation paid. See benefits table on page 70.

Receiving Benefit Payments

VA offers three methods for receiving benefit payments. More than 75 percent of veterans and beneficiaries receive their payments by direct deposit through an electronic fund transfer to their bank, savings and loan or credit union accounts. In some areas, benefit recipients who do not have an account at a financial institution may open a federally insured Electronic Transfer Account, which costs about $3 a month, provides a monthly statement and allows cash withdrawals. Recipients may also choose to receive benefits by check. To choose a payment method, veterans and beneficiaries should call VA's toll-free Helpline at 1-877-838-2778, Monday through Friday, 7:30 a.m. 4:00 p.m., Central Standard Time.

Prisoners of War

Former prisoners of war who were incarcerated for at least 30 days are presumed to be eligible for disability compensation if they become at least 10 percent disabled from diseases associated with POWs. These presumptive diseases are avitaminosis, beriberi heart disease and ischemic heart disease, chronic dysentery, helminthiasis, malnutrition including optic atrophy, pellagra and other nutritional deficiencies, psychosis, anxiety states and dysthymic disorder or depressive neurosis, post-traumatic osteoarthritis, irritable bowel syndrome, peptic ulcer disease, peripheral neuropathy and residuals of cold injury to include arthritis, neuropathy and skin cancer at the site of the cold injury.

Agent Orange and Other Herbicides

Nine diseases are presumed by VA to be service-related for compensation purposes for veterans exposed to Agent Orange and other herbicides. The diseases presumed are chloracne, porphyria cutanea tarda, soft-tissue sarcoma, Hodgkin's disease, multiple myeloma, respiratory cancers (lung, bronchus, larynx, trachea), non-Hodgkin's lymphoma, prostate cancer and acute and subacute peripheral neuropathy. Military personnel who served in Vietnam between Jan. 9, 1962, and May 5, 1975, are presumed to have been exposed to herbicides.

Veterans Exposed to Radiation

Veterans exposed to ionizing radiation while on active duty may be eligible for disability compensation if they have disabilities related to that exposure. To determine service-connection, factors considered include amount of radiation exposure, duration of exposure and elapsed time between exposure and onset of the disease. Conditions presumed to be service connected are all forms of leukemia except for chronic lymphocytic leukemia; cancer of the thyroid, breast, pharynx, esophagus, stomach, small intestine, pancreas, bile ducts, gall bladder, salivary gland, urinary tract, bronchiolo-alveolar carcinoma, multiple myeloma, primary liver cancer and lymphomas other than Hodgkin's disease.

Gulf War Veterans

Gulf War veterans who suffer from chronic disabilities resulting from undiagnosed illnesses may receive disability compensation. The undiagnosed illnesses must have appeared either during active duty in the Southwest Asia Theater of Operations during the Gulf War or at any time since then through Dec. 31, 2001.

The following symptoms may be manifestations of an undiagnosed illness: fatigue, skin disorders, headache, muscle pain, joint pain, neurologic symptoms, neuropsychological symptoms, symptoms involving the respiratory system, sleep disturbances, gastrointestinal symptoms, cardiovascular symptoms, abnormal weight loss and menstrual disorders. A disability is considered chronic if it has existed for at least six months.

Allowances for Dependents

Veterans whose service-connected disabilities are rated at 30 percent or more are entitled to additional allowances for dependents. The additional amount is determined according to the number of dependents and the degree of disability. A disabled veteran evaluated 30 percent or more also is entitled to receive a special allowance for a spouse who is in need of the aid and attendance of another person.

Incarcerated Veterans

VA benefits are restricted if a veteran, surviving spouse, child or dependent parent is convicted of a felony and imprisoned for more than 60 days. The disability compensation paid to a veteran incarcerated is limited to the 10 percent disability rate. For a surviving spouse, child, dependent parent or veteran whose disability rating is 10 percent, the payment is at the 5 percent rate. Any amounts not paid may be apportioned to eligible dependents. Payments are not reduced when the recipient is participating in a work-release program, residing in a halfway house or under community control. Overpayments for failure to notify VA of a veteran's incarceration result in the loss of all financial benefits until the overpayment is recovered.

Other Disability Benefits

Specially Adapted Homes

Disabled veterans may be entitled to a grant from VA for a home specially adapted to their needs or for adaptations to a house.

For a $43,000 Grant. VA may approve a grant of not more than 50 percent of the cost of building, buying or remodeling adapted homes or paying indebtedness on those homes already acquired, up to a maximum of $43,000. Veterans must be entitled to compensation for permanent and total service-connected disability due to:

    1. loss or loss of use of both lower extremities, such as to preclude locomotion without the aid of braces, crutches, canes or a wheelchair, or

    2. disability that includes (a) blindness in both eyes, having only light perception, plus (b) loss or loss of use of one lower extremity, or

3. loss or loss of use of one lower extremity together with (a) residuals of organic disease or injury, or (b) the loss or loss of use of one upper extremity, which so affects the functions of balance or propulsion as to preclude locomotion without using braces, canes, crutches or a wheelchair.

For a $8,250 Grant. VA may approve a grant for the actual cost, up to a maximum of $8,250, for adaptations to a veteran's residence that are determined by VA to be reasonably necessary. The grant also may be used to assist veterans in acquiring a residence that already has been adapted with special features for the veteran's disability. Veterans must be entitled to compensation for permanent and total service-connected disability due to (1) blindness in both eyes with 5/200 visual acuity or less, or (2) anatomical loss or loss of use of both hands.

Supplemental Financing. Veterans with available loan guaranty entitlement may also obtain a guaranteed loan or a direct loan from VA to supplement the grant to acquire a specially adapted home.

Automobile Assistance
Veterans and servicemembers qualify for this benefit if they have service-connected loss of one or both hands or feet, or permanent loss of use, or permanent impairment of vision of both eyes. Veterans entitled to compensation for ankylosis (immobility) of one or both knees, or one or both hips, also qualify for adaptive equipment for an automobile. There is a onetime payment by VA of not more than $8,000 toward the purchase of an automobile or other conveyance. VA will pay for adaptive equipment, and for repair, replacement, or reinstallation required because of disability, and for the safe operation of a vehicle purchased with VA assistance. To apply, contact a VA regional office or a VA medical center.

Clothing Allowance
Any veteran who is entitled to receive compensation for a service-connected disability for which he or she uses prosthetic or ortho-pedic appliances may receive an annual clothing allowance. The allowance also is available to any veteran whose service-connected skin condition requires prescribed medication that damages the veteran's outer garments. To apply, contact a VA regional office.

Pension

Veterans with low incomes may be eligible for monetary support if they have 90 days or more of active military service, one day of which was during a period of war. The discharge from active duty must have been under conditions other than dishonorable. The veteran must be permanently and totally disabled for reasons other than the veteran's own willful misconduct. Payments are made to qualified veterans to bring their total income, including other retirement or Social Security income, to a level set by Congress. Countable income may be reduced by unreimbursed medical expenses.

Improved Pension

The Improved Pension program provides for the maximum annual rates listed in the table on page 70. The payment is reduced by the amount of the countable income of the veteran and the income of the spouse or dependent children. When a veteran without a spouse or a child is being furnished nursing-home or domiciliary care by VA, the pension is reduced to an amount not to exceed $90 per month after three calendar months of care. The reduction may be delayed if nursing-home care is being continued for the primary purpose of providing the veteran with rehabilitation services.

Protected Pension Programs

Pensioners entitled to benefits as of Dec. 31, 1978, who do not elect to receive a pension under the Improved Pension program, continue to receive pension benefits at the rate they were entitled to receive on Dec. 31, 1978, as long as they remain permanently and totally disabled, do not lose a dependent, and their incomes do not exceed the income limitation, adjusted annually.

Aid and Attendance or Housebound

A veteran who is a patient in a nursing home, who is otherwise determined by VA to be in need of the regular aid and attendance of another person or who is permanently housebound, may be entitled to higher income limitations or additional benefits, depending on the type of pension received.

Medal of Honor Pension

VA administers pensions to holders of the Medal of Honor. In December 1998, Congress set the monthly pension at $600.

Incarcerated Veterans

A veteran while incarcerated may not receive VA pension benefits. The veteran's dependents, however, may receive a portion of such benefits. Failure to notify VA of a veteran's incarceration will cause the loss of all financial benefits until any overpayment is recovered.

Education and Training

Montgomery GI Bill (Active Duty)
Eligibility
The Montgomery GI Bill (Active Duty) provides a program of education benefits to individuals who enter active duty for the first time after June 30, 1985, and receive an honorable discharge. Active duty includes certain full-time National Guard duty performed after June 30, 1985. To receive the maximum benefit, the participant must serve on active duty for three continuous years. An individual also may qualify for the full benefit by initially serving two continuous years on active duty, followed by four years of Selected Reserve service, beginning within one year of release from active duty.

To participate in the Montgomery GI Bill (MGIB), servicemembers have their military pay reduced by $100 a month for the first 12 months of active duty. This money is not refundable. The participant generally must have a high school diploma or an equivalency certificate before the first period of active duty ends. Completing a minimum of 12 credit hours toward a college degree meets this requirement. Credits granted by colleges for life experiences may be used to meet this requirement. Individuals who serve a continuous period of at least three years of active duty, even though they were initially obligated to serve less, will be paid the maximum benefit.

Benefits under this program generally end 10 years from the date of the veteran's last discharge or release from active duty, but some extenuating circumstances qualify for extensions. A veteran with a discharge upgraded by the military will have 10 years from the date of the upgrade.

Vietnam Era GI Bill Conversions and other MGIB Enrollment
Also eligible for Montgomery GI Bill benefits are individuals who had remaining entitlement under the Vietnam Era GI Bill on Dec. 31, 1989, and served on active duty between Oct. 19, 1984, and July 1, 1985, and continued to serve on active duty to July 1, 1988, or to

July 1, 1987, followed by four years in the Selected Reserve. An individual who converts from the Vietnam Era GI Bill must have had a high school diploma or an equivalency certificate before Dec. 31, 1989. Completion of 12 credit hours toward a college degree meets this requirement. Certain other individuals who are involuntarily separated from active duty after Feb. 2, 1991, may receive MGIB benefits, but they must agree to have their basic pay reduced by $1,200. Additionally, individuals who voluntarily separated on or after Oct. 23, 1992, under the Voluntary Separation Incentive or the Special Separation Benefit programs may participate in the MGIB program if they agreed to have their basic pay reduced by $1,200.

Discharges and Separations

For the Montgomery GI Bill program, the discharge must be honorable. Discharges designated "under honorable conditions" and "general" do not establish eligibility. An honorable discharge for one of the following reasons may result in a reduction of the required length of active duty: (1) convenience of the government; (2) disability; (3) hardship; (4) a medical condition existing before service; (5) force reductions; (6) physical or mental conditions which prevent satisfactory performance of duty.

Education and Training Available

The following are available under the Montgomery GI Bill: (1) Courses at colleges and universities leading to associate, bachelor or graduate degrees, and accredited independent study; (2) Courses leading to a certificate or diploma from business, technical or vocational schools; (3) Apprenticeship or on-job training programs for individuals not on active duty; (4) Correspondence courses, under certain conditions; (5) Flight training, if the veteran has a private pilot license and meets the medical requirements upon beginning the training program; (6) Tutorial assistance benefits if the individual is enrolled in school halftime or more, and refresher, deficiency and similar training; (7) State-approved teacher certification programs; (8) Preparatory courses necessary for admission to a college or graduate school.

Work-Study

Participants may be paid a work-study allowance if they train at the three-quarter or full-time rate. They may elect to be paid in advance a portion of the allowance equal to 40 percent of the total. Participants under the supervision of a VA employee may provide VA outreach services, prepare and process VA paperwork, and work at a VA medical facility or perform other VA approved activities.

Counseling

Educational and vocational counseling may be available for individuals who are eligible for VA educational assistance; who are on active duty and within 180 days of discharge; or who have been discharged one year or less. VA will help individuals understand their educational and vocational needs, and plan an educational or vocational goal. VA also may help individuals plan a job search.

Payments

Veterans who served on active duty for three years or more, or two years active duty plus four years in the Selected Reserve or National Guard, will receive $536 a month in basic benefits for 36 months. Those who enlist and serve for less than three years will receive $436 a month. VA will pay an additional amount, commonly called a "kicker," if directed by the Defense Department.

Montgomery GI Bill (Selected Reserve)
Eligibility

The Montgomery GI Bill (Selected Reserve) provides education benefits to members of the reserve elements of the Army, Navy, Air Force, Marine Corps and Coast Guard, and to members of the Army National Guard and the Air National Guard. To be eligible for the program, a reservist must: (1) have a six-year obligation to serve in the Selected Reserve signed after June 30, 1985, or, if an officer, agree to serve six years in addition to the original obligation; (2) complete Initial Active Duty for Training (IADT); (3) have a high school diploma or equivalency certificate before completing IADT; and (4) remain in good standing in a Selected Reserve unit.

Education and Training Available

Reservists may seek an undergraduate degree, go for graduate training, or take technical courses at colleges and universities. Flight training also is allowed. Those who have a six-year commitment beginning after Sept. 30, 1990, may take courses for a certificate or diploma from business, technical or vocational schools; cooperative training; apprenticeship or on-job training; correspondence courses; independent study programs; flight training; tutorial assistance; remedial, refresher and other training; and state-approved certification programs for training alternate teachers.

Period of Eligibility

If a reservist stays in the Selected Reserve, benefits end 10 years from the date the reservist became eligible for the program. VA may extend the 10-year period if the individual could not train due to a disability caused by Selected Reserve service. If a reservist leaves the Selected Reserve because of a disability, the individual may use the full 10 years. VA may also extend the 10-year period if the reservist was ordered to active duty. In other cases, benefits end the day the reservist leaves the Selected Reserve, except that certain individuals separated from the Selected Reserve due to downsizing of the military between Oct. 1, 1991, and Sept. 30, 1999, will have the full 10 years to use their benefits. If the 10-year period ends while the participant is attending school, however, VA will pay benefits until the end of the term. If the training is not on a term basis, payments may continue for 12 weeks.

Work-Study
Participants may be paid a work-study allowance if they train at the three-quarter or full-time rate. They may elect to be paid in advance a portion of the allowance equal to 40 percent of the total. Participants under the supervision of a VA employee may provide VA outreach services, prepare and process VA paperwork, and work at a VA medical facility or perform other VA approved activities.

Counseling
Educational and vocational counseling may be available for individuals who are eligible for VA educational assistance; who are on active duty and within 180 days of discharge; or who have been discharged one year or less. VA will help these individuals understand their educational and vocational strengths and weaknesses and plan an educational or vocational goal. VA also may help individuals plan a job search.

Payments
The full-time rate is $255 a month for 36 months.

Veterans' Educational Assistance Program (VEAP)
Eligibility
Under VEAP, active duty personnel voluntarily participated in a plan for education or training in which their savings were administered and added to by the federal government. Servicepersons were eligible to enroll in VEAP if they entered active duty for the first time after Dec. 31, 1976, and before July 1, 1985. Some contribution to VEAP must have been made prior to April 1, 1987. The maximum participant contribution is $2,700. While on active duty, participants may make a lump-sum contribution to the training fund.

A serviceperson who participated in VEAP is eligible to receive benefits while on active duty if: (1) at least three months of contributions are available, except for high school or elementary school, in which case only one month of contributions is needed; and (2) the first active-duty commitment is completed. If the individual's first term is for more than six years, benefits may be available after six years. To attend an elementary or high school program, the individual must be in the last six months of the first enlistment.

A veteran who participated in VEAP is eligible to receive benefits if the discharge was under conditions other than dishonorable on or after Jan. 1, 1977, and served for a continuous period of 181 days or more, or was discharged for a service-connected disability.

Education eligibility may be established even though the required active duty is not completed if the veteran was discharged or released for a service-connected disability.

Education and Training Available
VEAP participants may pursue associate, bachelor or graduate degrees at colleges or universities. Courses leading to a certificate or diploma from business, technical or vocational schools may also be taken. Other opportunities may include apprenticeship or on-job training programs; cooperative courses; correspondence courses; tutorial assistance; refresher, deficiency and other training; and state-approved alternative teacher certification programs.

Flight training also may be pursued, including solo flying hours up to the minimum required by the FAA for the rating or certification being pursued. Before beginning training, the veteran must have a private pilot license and meet the medical requirements for a commercial license throughout the training program.

A participant may study abroad in programs leading to a college degree and in programs which offer, as part of the curriculum, nontraditional training away from school. A participant with a deficiency in a subject may receive tutorial assistance benefits if enrolled halftime or more.

Period of Eligibility
A veteran has 10 years from the date of last discharge or release from active duty to use VEAP benefits. This 10-year period can be extended by the amount of time the veteran could not train because

of a disability or because of being held by a foreign government or power. The 10-year period may also be extended if the veteran re-enters active duty for 90 continuous days or more after becoming eligible. For periods of less than 90 days, the veteran may qualify for extensions under certain circumstances. The extension ends 10 years from the date of discharge or release from the later active duty period. A veteran with a discharge upgraded by the military will have 10 years from the date of the upgrade.

Work-Study
Participants may be paid a work-study allowance if they train at the three-quarter or full-time rate. They may elect to be paid in advance a portion of the allowance equal to 40 percent of the total. Participants under the supervision of a VA employee may provide VA outreach services, prepare and process VA paperwork, and work at a VA medical facility or perform other VA approved activities.

Counseling
Educational and vocational counseling may be available for veterans who are eligible for VA educational assistance; who are on active duty and within 180 days of discharge; or who have been discharged one year or less. VA will help individuals understand their educational and vocational needs and help plan an educational or vocational goal. VA also may help in the search for a job.

Payments
When the participant elects to use VEAP benefits, the Defense Department will match the participant's contribution at the rate of $2 for every $1 the individual put into the fund. Defense also may make additional contributions to the fund in exchange for special duties performed by the participant.

Vocational Rehabilitation and Employment

Vocational Rehabilitation and Employment is an employment-oriented program that assists veterans with service-connected disabilities by offering them services and assistance to help them prepare for, find and keep suitable employment. Suitable employment is work that is within the veterans' physical and emotional capabilities and matches their patterns of skills, abilities and interests. For veterans whose disabilities make employment unlikely, VA helps them attain as much daily living independence as possible.

Services
Depending on an individual's needs, services provided by VA may include:
1. an evaluation of the individual's abilities, skills and interests
2. assistance finding and maintaining suitable employment
3. vocational counseling and planning
4. training, such as on-the-job and work experience programs
5. training, such as certificate, two, or four-year college or technical programs
6. supportive rehabilitation services and additional counseling.

VA pays the cost of these services and pays a living allowance to veterans who participate in a training program.

Eligibility
A veteran must have a VA established service-connected disability of at least 10 percent with a serious employment handicap or 20 percent with an employment handicap and be discharged or released from military service under other than dishonorable conditions. A servicemember pending medical separation from active duty may apply, but the disability rating must be at least 20 percent.

Entitlement
Eligible veterans are evaluated to determine if vocational rehabilitation services are needed to help overcome barriers to employment.

Period of a Rehabilitation Program
Generally, veterans must complete a vocational rehabilitation program within 12 years of separation from military service or within 12 years of compensable service-connected disability award notification by VA. Depending on the length of program needed, veterans may be provided up to 48 months of full-time services or their part-time equivalent. These limitations may be extended in certain circumstances.

Work Study
Participants may be paid a work-study allowance if they train at the three-quarter or full-time rate. They may elect to be paid in advance a portion of the allowance equal to 40 percent of the total. Participants under the supervision of a VA employee may provide VA outreach services, prepare and process VA paperwork, and work at a VA medical facility or perform other VA approved activities.

Vocational Training for Children with Spina Bifida

The Vocational Rehabilitation and Employment program administers a vocational training program to enable a qualified child to prepare for and attain suitable employment. Services may include counseling and rehabilitative services, education, training and employment services leading to suitable employment. VA pays for the cost of these services.

Eligibility

To qualify for entitlement to a vocational training program, an applicant must be a child:

1. to whom VA has awarded a monthly allowance for spina bifida; and

2. for whom VA has determined that achievement of a vocational goal is reasonably feasible.

A vocational training program may not begin before a child's 18th birthday or the date of completion of secondary schooling, whichever comes first. Depending on the need, a child may be provided up to 24 months of full-time training.

Program for Unemployable Veterans

Veterans awarded 100 percent disability compensation based upon unemployability may still request an evaluation and, if found eligible, may participate in a vocational rehabilitation program and receive help in getting a job. A veteran who secures employment under the special program will continue to receive 100 percent disability compensation until the veteran has worked continuously for at least 12 months.

Home Loan Guaranties

VA loan guaranties are made to servicemembers, veterans, reservists and unremarried surviving spouses for the purchase of homes, condominiums and manufactured homes and for refinancing loans. VA guarantees part of the total loan, permitting the purchaser to obtain a mortgage with a competitive interest rate, even without a down payment if the lender agrees. VA requires that a down payment be made for the purchase of a manufactured home. VA also requires a down payment for a home or condominium if the purchase price exceeds the reasonable value of the property or the loan has a graduated payment feature. With a VA guaranty, the lender is protected against loss up to the amount of the guaranty if the borrower fails to repay the loan. A VA loan guaranty can be used to:

1. Buy a home.
2. Buy a residential condominium.
3. Build a home.
4. Repair, alter or improve a home.
5. Refinance an existing home loan.
6. Buy a manufactured home with or without a lot.
7. Buy and improve a manufactured home lot.
8. Install a solar heating or cooling system or other weather-ization improvements.
9. Purchase and improve a home simultaneously with energy-efficient improvements.
10. Refinance an existing VA loan to reduce the interest rate and make energy-efficient improvements.
11. Refinance a manufactured home loan to acquire a lot.

Eligibility

Applicants must have a good credit rating, have an income sufficient to support mortgage payments, and agree to live in the property. To obtain a VA Certificate of Eligibility, complete VA Form 26-1880, Request for a Certificate of Eligibility for VA Home Loan Benefits, and mail it to one of the two VA Eligibility Centers (Winston-Salem and Los Angeles). In general, those veterans living in the Western part of the country mail their applications to the Los Angeles Eligibility Center, while those living in the Eastern part of the country mail applications to Winston-Salem. You can find more information on eligibility and addresses for the Centers by contacting your local VA office or by visiting www.vba.va.gov/bln/loan/elig.htm on the World Wide Web.

World War II: (1) active duty service after Sept. 15, 1940, and prior to July 26, 1947; (2) discharge under other than dishonorable conditions; and (3) at least 90 days service unless discharged early for service-connected disability.

Post-World War II: (1) active duty service after July 25, 1947, and prior to June 27, 1950; (2) discharge under other than dishonorable conditions; and (3) 181 days continuous active duty unless discharged early for service-connected disability.

Korean Conflict: (1) active duty after June 26, 1950, and prior to

Feb. 1, 1955; (2) discharge under other than dishonorable conditions; and (3) at least 90 days total service, unless discharged early for service-connected disability.

Post-Korean Conflict: (1) active duty between Jan. 31, 1955, and Aug. 5, 1964; (2) discharge under conditions other than dishonorable; (3) 181 days continuous service, unless discharged early for service-connected disability.

Vietnam: (1) Active duty after Aug. 4, 1964, and prior to May 8, 1975; (2) discharge under conditions other than dishonorable; and (3) 90 days total service, unless discharged early for service-connected disability. For veterans who served in the Republic of Vietnam, the beginning date is Feb. 28, 1961.

Post-Vietnam: For veterans whose enlisted service began before Sept. 8, 1980, or whose service as an officer began before Oct. 17, 1981: (1) active duty for 181 continuous days, all of which occurred after May 7, 1975, and discharge under conditions other than dishonorable; or (2) early discharge for service-connected disability. For veterans separated from enlisted service between Sept. 8, 1980, and Aug. 1, 1990, or service as an officer between Oct. 17, 1981, and Aug. 1, 1990: (1) completion of 24 months of continuous active duty or the full period — at least 181 days — for which the person was called or ordered to active duty, and discharge under conditions other than dishonorable; or (2) completion of at least 181 days of active duty with a hardship discharge or discharge for the convenience of the government, reduction-in-force or certain medical conditions; or (3) early discharge for service-connected disability.

Gulf War: (1) completion of 24 months of continuous active duty or the full period — at least 90 days — for which the person was called to active duty, and discharge from active duty under conditions other than dishonorable; or (2) discharge after at least 90 days with a hardship discharge, discharge at the convenience of the government, reduction-in-force or certain medical conditions, or discharge for service-connected disability. Reservists and National Guard members are eligible if they were activated after Aug. 1, 1990, served at least 90 days, and were discharged honorably.

Active Duty Personnel: Until the Gulf War era is ended by law or Presidential Proclamation, persons on active duty are eligible after serving on continuous active duty for 90 days.

Members of the Selected Reserve: Individuals are eligible if they have completed at least six years in the reserves or National Guard or were discharged because of a service-connected disability. This eligibility expires September 30, 2007. Reservists who do not qualify for VA housing loan benefits may be eligible for loans on favorable terms insured by the Federal Housing Administration (FHA) of the Department of Housing and Urban Development (HUD).

Others: Others eligible include unremarried spouses of veterans or reservists who died on active duty or as a result of service-connected causes; spouses of active-duty servicemembers who have been missing in action or a prisoner of war for at least 90 days; U.S. citizens who served in the armed forces of a U.S. ally in World War II; and members of organizations with recognized contributions to the U.S. World War II effort. Eligibility may be determined at the VA Eligibility Centers.

Guaranty Amount

The amount of the VA guaranty available to an eligible veteran is called the entitlement and may be considered the equivalent of a down payment by lenders. Up to $50,750 in entitlement may be available to veterans purchasing or constructing homes to be financed with a loan of more than $144,000 and to veterans who obtain an Interest Rate Reduction Refinancing Loan of more than $144,000. The amount of entitlement varies with the loan amount. Loan guaranty limits are listed in a table on page 74.

VA does not establish a maximum loan amount. No loan for the acquisition of a home, however, may exceed the reasonable value of the property. A loan for the purpose of refinancing existing mortgage loans or other liens secured on a dwelling is generally limited to 90 percent of the appraised value of the dwelling. A loan to reduce the interest rate on an existing VA-guaranteed loan, however, can be made for an amount equal to the outstanding balance on the old loan plus closing costs, up to two discount points, and energy-efficient improvements. A loan for the purchase of a manufactured home or lot is limited to 95 percent of the amount that would be subject to finance charges. The VA funding fee and up to $6,000 in energy-efficient improvements also may be included in the loan. A veteran who previously obtained a VA loan can use the remaining entitlement for a second purchase. The amount of remaining entitlement is the difference between $36,000 ($50,750 for special loans) and the amount of entitlement used on prior loans. Veterans refinancing an existing VA loan with a new VA loan at a lower interest rate need not have any entitlement available for use.

Required Occupancy

Veterans must certify that they intend to live in the home they are buying or building with a VA guaranty. A veteran who wishes to refinance or improve a home with a VA guaranty also must certify to being in occupancy at the time of application. A spouse may certify occupancy if the buyer is on active duty. In refinancing a VA-guaranteed loan solely to reduce the interest rate, veterans need only certify to prior occupancy.

Closing Costs

Payment in cash is required on all home loan closing costs, including title search and recording, hazard insurance premiums, prepaid taxes and a 1 percent origination fee, which may be required by lenders in lieu of certain other costs. In the case of refinancing loans, all such costs may be included in the loan, as long as the total loan does not exceed 90 percent of the reasonable value of the property. Interest Rate Reduction Refinancing Loans may include closing costs and a maximum of 2 discount points. Loans, including refinancing loans, are charged a funding fee by VA, except for loans made to disabled veterans and unremarried surviving spouses of veterans who died as a result of service. The VA funding fee is based on the loan amount and, at the discretion of the veteran and the lender, may be included in the loan. Funding fee rates are listed in a table on page 74.

Financing, Interest Rates and Terms

Veterans obtain VA-guaranteed loans through the usual lending institutions, including banks, savings and loan associations, building and loan associations, and mortgage loan companies. Veterans may obtain a loan with a fixed interest rate, which may be negotiated with the lender. If the lender charges discount points on the loan, the veteran may negotiate with the seller as to who will pay points or if they will be split between buyer and seller. Points paid by the veteran may not be included in the loan, except that a maximum of 2 points may be included in Interest Rate Reduction Refinancing Loans. The loan may be for as long as 30 years and 32 days.
VA does not require that a down payment be made, except in the following instances: 1) a manufactured home or lot loan; 2) a loan with graduated payment features; and 3) to prevent the amount of a loan from exceeding VA's determination of the property's reasonable

value. If the sale price exceeds the reasonable value, the veteran must certify that the difference is being paid in cash without supplementary borrowing. A cash down payment of 5 percent of the purchase price is required for manufactured home or lot loans.

Release of Liability, Loan Assumption

When a veteran sells a home financed through a VA guaranty to a purchaser who assumes the loan, the veteran may request release from liability to the federal government provided the loan is current, the purchaser has been obligated by contract to purchase the property and assume all of the veteran's liabilities, and VA is satisfied that the purchaser is a good risk. A release of liability does not mean that a veteran's guaranty entitlement is restored.   If the new veteran-buyer agrees to substitute entitlement for that of the veteran-seller, entitlement may be restored to the veteran-seller.

A VA loan for which a commitment was made on or after March 1, 1988, is not assumable without approval of VA or its authorized agent. The person who assumes a VA loan for which a commitment was made on or after March 1, 1988, must pay a fee to VA equal to 1/2 of 1 percent of the balance of the loan being assumed. If a person disposes of the property securing a VA-guaranteed loan for which a commitment was made after March 1, 1988, without first notifying the holder of the loan, the holder may demand immediate and full payment of the loan. Veterans whose loans were closed after December 31, 1989, have no liability to the government following a foreclosure, except in cases involving fraud, misrepresentation or bad faith.

Loans for Native Americans

VA direct home loans are available to eligible Native American veterans who wish to purchase, construct or improve a home on Native American trust land. These loans may be used to simultaneously purchase and improve a home. Direct loans also are available to reduce the interest rate on existing loans obtained under this program. VA direct loans may be limited to the cost of the home or $80,000, whichever is less. A funding fee must be paid to VA. The fee is 1.25 percent for loans to purchase, construct or improve a home. For loans to refinance an existing loan, the fee is 0.5 percent of the loan amount. Veterans receiving compensation for service-connected disability are not required to pay the funding fee. Veterans who qualify based on non-active duty service in the Reserves or National Guard are charged a funding fee of 2 percent of the loan amount. The funding fee may be paid in cash or included in the loan. The following may not be included in the loan: VA appraisal, credit report, loan processing fee, title search, title insurance, recording fees, transfer taxes, survey charges or hazard insurance.

Repossessed Homes
VA sells homes that have been acquired after foreclosure of a VA-guaranteed loan. These homes are available to both veterans and nonveterans. Contact local real estate agents for available listings.

Safeguards for Veterans
1.   Homes completed less than a year before purchase with VA financing and inspected during construction by either VA or HUD must meet VA requirements.

2.   VA may suspend from the loan program those who take unfair advantage of veteran borrowers or decline to sell a new home or make a loan because of race, color, religion, sex, disability, family status or national origin.

3.   The builder of a new home is required to give the purchasing veteran a one-year warranty that the home has been constructed to VA-approved plans and specifications. A similar warranty must be given for new manufactured homes.

4.   In cases of new construction completed under VA or HUD inspection, VA may pay or otherwise compensate the veteran borrower for correction of structural defects seriously affecting livability if assistance is requested within four years of a home-loan guaranty.

5.   The borrower obtaining a loan may only be charged the fees and other charges prescribed by VA as allowable.

6.   The borrower can prepay without penalty the entire loan or any part not less than the amount of one installment or $100.

7.   VA encourages holders to extend forbearance if a borrower becomes temporarily unable to meet the terms of the loan.

Life Insurance

Two regular and two disabled insurance programs are currently open for new policyholders. Servicemembers' Group Life Insurance is open to active-duty members and reservists of the uniformed services. Veterans' Group Life Insurance is available to individuals released from active duty after Aug. 1, 1974, and to separated reservists. Service-Disabled Insurance is available for veterans with service-connected disabilities. Veterans' Mortgage Life Insurance provides mortgage life insurance for veterans who are eligible for specially adapted housing grants.

Servicemembers' Group Life Insurance
The following are automatically insured for $200,000 under Servicemembers' Group Life Insurance (SGLI): active-duty members of the Army, Navy, Air Force, Marines and Coast Guard; commissioned members of the National Oceanic and Atmospheric Administration and the Public Health Service; cadets or midshipmen of the service academies; members, cadets and midshipmen of the ROTC while engaged in authorized training; and members of the Ready Reserves. Individuals may elect to be covered for a lesser amount or not to be covered at all. Part-time coverage may be provided to members of the Reserves who do not qualify for full-time coverage. Premiums are deducted automatically from an individual's pay or are collected by the individual's service branch.

Veterans' Group Life Insurance
SGLI may be converted to Veterans' Group Life Insurance (VGLI), which is renewable five-year term coverage. This program is administered by the Office of Servicemembers' Group Life Insurance (OSGLI), 213 Washington St., Newark, NJ 07102. VGLI is available to: (a) individuals with full-time SGLI coverage upon release from active duty or the Reserves; (b) individuals with part-time SGLI coverage who incur a disability or aggravate a pre-existing disability during a reserve period which renders them uninsurable at standard premium rates; and (c) members of the Individual Ready Reserve and Inactive National Guard.

Individuals entitled to SGLI coverage can convert to VGLI by submitting the premium within 120 days of separating from active duty or the reserves. After 121 days, the individual may be granted VGLI provided initial premium and evidence of insurability are submitted within one year after termination of the individual's SGLI coverage. Individuals with full-time SGLI coverage who are totally disabled at the time of separation and whose service makes them eligible for VGLI may purchase the insurance while remaining totally disabled up to one year following separation.

Service-Disabled Veterans Insurance
A veteran who has a service-connected disability but is otherwise in good health may apply to VA for up to $10,000 in life insurance coverage at standard insurance rates within two years from the date

of being notified of service-connected status. This insurance is limited to veterans who left service after April 24, 1951. Veterans who are totally disabled may apply for a waiver of premiums. For those veterans who are eligible for this waiver, additional coverage of up to $20,000 is available. Premiums cannot be waived on the additional insurance.

Veterans' Mortgage Life Insurance

The maximum amount of mortgage life insurance available for those who are eligible for a specially adapted housing grant is $90,000. Protection is automatic unless the veteran declines. Premiums are automatically deducted from VA benefit payments or paid direct, if the veteran does not draw compensation, and will continue until the mortgage has been liquidated, the home is sold, or the coverage terminates when the veteran reaches age 70. If a mortgage is disposed of, VMLI may be obtained on the mortgage of another home.

Insurance Dividends

Those insurance programs that pay dividends pay on the policy anniversary date. The Internal Revenue Service has announced that interest on insurance dividends left on deposit with VA is not taxable. For details on this ruling, contact the IRS.

Assistance with Insurance

Increasing Insurance. Policyholders with National Service Life Insurance, Veterans Special Life Insurance and Veterans Reopened Insurance can use their dividends to purchase additional paid-up coverage.

Reinstating Lapsed Insurance. Lapsed term policies may be reinstated within five years from the date of lapse. Contact the Insurance Center for details. A five-year term policy that is not lapsed at the end of the term period is automatically renewed for an additional five-year period.

Converting Term Policies. A term policy that is in force may be converted to a permanent plan. Upon reaching renewal at age 70 or older, National Service Life Insurance term policies on total disability premium waiver are automatically converted to permanent insurance, which provides cash, loan value and higher dividends.

Modified Life Policy. A "modified life at age 65" plan is available to National Service Life policyholders. The premium rates for this plan remain the same throughout the premium-paying period, while the face value reduces by 50 percent at age 65. The reduced amount may be replaced with a "special ordinary life." A "modified life at age 70" plan also is available.

Disability Provisions. National Service Life policyholders who become totally disabled should consult VA about premium waivers.

Borrowing on Policies. Policyholders may borrow up to 94 percent of the cash surrender value of their insurance and continue the insurance in force by payment of premiums. Interest on policy loans is compounded annually. The current interest rate may be obtained at any VA office, or by calling toll-free 1-800-669-8477.

For additional information about government life insurance, call the VA Insurance Center in Philadelphia toll-free, 1-800-669-8477. Specialists are available between the hours of 8:30 a.m. and 6 p.m., Eastern Time, to discuss premium payments, insurance dividends, changes of address, policy loans, naming beneficiaries and reporting the death of the insured. After hours, a caller may leave a recorded message to be answered on the next workday. If the policy number is unknown, send the veteran's VA file number, date of birth, Social Security number, military serial number or military service branch and dates of service to:

> Department of Veterans Affairs
> Regional Office and Insurance Center
> Box 42954
> Philadelphia, PA 19101

Burial Benefits

Burial in National Cemeteries

VA Cemeteries

Burial benefits in a VA national cemetery include the gravesite, a headstone or marker, opening and closing of the grave, and perpetual care. Many national cemeteries have columbaria or gravesites for cremated remains. To contact a cemetery, see the "VA Facilities" section in the back of this book.

Veterans and servicemembers are eligible for burial in a VA national cemetery. An eligible veteran must have been discharged or separated from active duty under conditions other than dishonorable and have completed the required period of service. Persons entitled to retired pay as a result of 20 years creditable service with a reserve component are eligible. A U.S. citizen who served in the armed forces of a government allied with the United States in a war also may be eligible. A 1997 law bars certain persons convicted of federal or state capital crimes who are sentenced to death or life without parole from being buried or memorialized in one of the VA national cemeteries or in Arlington National Cemetery.

Spouses and minor children of eligible veterans and of servicemembers also may be buried in a national cemetery. Certain adult children incapable of self support due to physical or mental disability are eligible for burial. If a surviving spouse of an eligible veteran marries a nonveteran, and remarriage was terminated by annulment, divorce or the death of the nonveteran, the spouse is eligible for burial in a national cemetery.

Gravesites in national cemeteries cannot be reserved. Funeral directors or others making burial arrangements must apply at the time of death. Reservations made under previous programs are honored. By law, the Department of Defense is the government agency responsible for providing military funeral honors. Honors are normally arranged by the family or funeral home; staff at national cemeteries may make referrals to military units or volunteer groups. The National Cemetery Administration normally does not conduct burials on weekends. A weekend caller, however, will be directed to one of three VA cemetery offices that remain open during weekends to schedule burials at the cemetery of the caller's choice during the following week.

Arlington National Cemetery
Arlington National Cemetery is under the jurisdiction of the Army. Eligibility for burials is more limited than at other national cemeteries. For information on Arlington burials, write to Superintendent, Arlington National Cemetery, Arlington, VA 22211, or call 703-695-3250.

Interior Department, State Veterans Cemeteries
The two active national cemeteries administered by the Department of the Interior are Andersonville National Cemetery in Georgia and Andrew Johnson National Cemetery in Tennessee. Eligibility for burial is similar to VA cemetery eligibility. Cemeteries for veterans also are operated by many states. For burials in these cemeteries, contact the cemetery or the applicable state.

Headstones and Markers
VA provides headstones and markers for the unmarked graves of veterans anywhere in the world and of eligible dependents of veterans buried in military post, state veteran or national cemeteries. Flat bronze, flat granite, flat marble, upright granite and upright marble types are available to mark the grave in a style consistent with the cemetery. Niche markers also are available for identifying cremated remains in columbaria.

Headstones and markers are inscribed with the name of the deceased, branch of service, and the years of birth and death. Optional items that may be inscribed are military grade, rank or rate; war service such as "World War II"; months and days of birth and death; an approved emblem of one's belief; and text indicating valor awards. When burial is in a military post, state veteran or national cemetery, the headstone or marker is ordered through the cemetery, which will place it on the grave. Information on style, inscription and shipping can be obtained from the cemetery.

When burial occurs in a cemetery other than a military post, state veteran or national cemetery, the headstone or marker must be applied for from VA. It is shipped at government expense. VA,

44

however, does not pay the cost of placing the headstone or marker. To apply, complete VA Form 40-1330 and forward it to Director, Memorial Programs Service (403A), Department of Veterans Affairs, 810 Vermont Ave., NW, Washington, DC 20420.

Forms and assistance are available at VA regional offices. For information regarding the status of an application, write to the Director, Memorial Programs Service (403A), or call 1-800-697-6947. VA cannot issue a headstone or marker for a spouse or child buried in a private cemetery. Twenty-year reservists generally are eligible for a headstone or grave marker.

Memorial Headstones or Markers

To memorialize an eligible veteran whose remains are not available for burial, VA will provide a memorial headstone or marker. The headstone or marker is the same as that used to identify a grave except that the phrase "In Memory of" precedes the inscription. The headstone or marker is available to memorialize eligible veterans or deceased servicemembers whose remains were not recovered or identified, were buried at sea, donated to science, or cremated and scattered. The memorial marker must be placed in a national, state veterans, local or private cemetery. In the case of placement in a state, local or private cemetery, VA supplies the marker and pays the cost of shipping, but does not pay for the plot or the placement of the headstone or marker.

Presidential Memorial Certificates

Presidential Memorial Certificates express the nation's recognition of a veteran's service. Certificates bearing the signature of the President are issued honoring deceased veterans with honorable discharges. Eligible recipients include next of kin and other loved ones. The award of a certificate to one eligible recipient does not preclude certificates to other eligible recipients. The veteran may have died at any time. To establish honorable service, a copy of a document such as a discharge, form DD-214, must accompany requests for a certificate. VA regional offices can assist in applying for certificates.

Military Funeral Honors

Upon request, the Department of Defense will provide military funeral honors for the burial of military members and eligible veterans. A basic military funeral honors ceremony consists of the folding and presentation of the American flag and the playing of Taps by a bugler, if available, or by electronic recording. A funeral honors detail to perform this ceremony consists of two or more uniformed members of the Armed Forces, with at least one member from the service in which the deceased veteran served.

Military members on active duty or in the Selected Reserve are eligible for military funeral honors. Also eligible are former military members who served on active duty and departed under conditions other than dishonorable, former members of the Selected Reserve who completed at least one term of enlistment or period of initial obligated service and departed under conditions other than dishonorable, and former military members discharged from the Selected Reserve due to a disability incurred or aggravated in the line of duty.

The Department of Defense maintains a toll-free telephone line (1-877-MIL-HONR) for use by Funeral Directors only to request honors. Family members should inform their funeral directors if they desire military funeral honors for a veteran. For more information, visit http://www.militaryfuneralhonors.osd.mil, the Department of Defense military funeral honors World Wide Web site.

Burial Flags
VA provides an American flag to drape the casket of a deceased individual who:
   1. served in any war,
   2. died while in the active military, naval, or air service after May 27, 1941,
   3. served after Jan. 31, 1955,
   4. died while a member of the Selected Reserve,
   5. served at least one enlistment or had been discharged or released from active service for a disability incurred or aggravated in the line of duty,
   6. was entitled to retired pay for service as a Reservist at the time of death, or would have been entitled to retired pay, but for the fact that the individual was under 60 years of age,
   7. was a member or former member of the Selected Reserve who completed at least one enlistment or period of initial obligated service as a member of the Selected Reserve, or was discharged before completion of the initial period for a disability incurred or aggravated in the line of duty.

Veterans separated from the service must have been discharged or released under conditions other than dishonorable. After the funeral service, the flag may be given to the next of kin, close friend or associate of the deceased veteran. Burial flags may be obtained at VA regional offices, national cemeteries and most local post offices.

Reimbursement of Burial Expenses

VA will pay a burial allowance up to $1,500 if the veteran's death is service-connected. In some instances, VA also will pay the cost of transporting the remains of a service-disabled veteran to the national cemetery nearest the home of the deceased that has available grave-sites. In such cases, the person who bore the veteran's burial expenses may claim reimbursement from VA.

VA will pay a $300 burial and funeral expense allowance for veterans who, at time of death, were entitled to receive pension or compensation or would have been entitled to compensation but for receipt of military retirement pay. Eligibility also may be established when death occurs in a VA facility, a nursing home under VA contract or a state veterans nursing home. Additional costs of transportation of the remains may be paid. There is no time limit for filing reimbursement claims of service-connected deaths. In other deaths, claims must be filed within two years after permanent burial or cremation.

VA will pay a $150 plot allowance when a veteran is not buried in a cemetery that is under U.S. government jurisdiction under the following circumstances: the veteran was discharged from active duty because of disability incurred or aggravated in the line of duty; the veteran was in receipt of compensation or pension or would have been except for receiving military retired pay; or the veteran died in a VA facility. The $150 plot allowance may be paid to the state if a veteran is buried without charge for the cost of a plot or interment in a state-owned cemetery reserved solely for veteran burials. Burial expenses paid by the deceased's employer or a state agency will not be reimbursed. For information on monetary benefits, call 1-800-827-1000.

Visit the National Cemetery Administration web site at www.cem.va.gov or call 1-800-827-1000 from any location in the United States for additional information on burial eligibility or other VA benefits.

BENEFITS FOR SURVIVORS

Dependency and Indemnity Compensation (DIC)

Dependency and Indemnity Compensation (DIC) payments may be available for surviving spouses who have not remarried, unmarried children under 18, helpless children, those between 18 and 23 if attending a VA-approved school, and low-income parents of deceased servicemembers or veterans. To be eligible, the deceased must have died from: (1) a disease or injury incurred or aggravated while on active duty or active duty for training; (2) an injury incurred or aggravated in line of duty while on inactive duty training; or (3) a disability compensable by VA. Death cannot be the result of willful misconduct. If a spouse remarries, eligibility for benefits may be restored if the marriage is terminated later by death or divorce.

DIC payments also may be authorized for survivors of veterans who were totally service-connected disabled at time of death but whose deaths were not the result of their service-connected disability. The survivor qualifies if: (1) the veteran was continuously rated totally disabled for a period of 10 or more years immediately preceding death; (2) the veteran was so rated for a period of at least five years from the date of military discharge; or (3) the veteran was a former prisoner of war who died after September 30, 1999, and who was continuously rated totally disabled for a period of at least one year immediately preceding death. Payments under this provision are subject to offset by the amount received from judicial proceedings brought on account of the veteran's death. The discharge must have been under conditions other than dishonorable.

DIC Payments to Surviving Spouse

Surviving spouses of veterans who died after Jan. 1, 1993, receive $881 a month. For a spouse entitled to DIC based on the veteran's death prior to Jan. 1, 1993, the amount paid is $881 or an amount based on the veteran's pay grade as given in the table on page 72.

DIC Payments to Parents and Children

The monthly payment for parents of deceased veterans depends upon their income. There are additional DIC payments for dependent children. A child may be eligible if there is no surviving spouse, and the child is unmarried and under age 18, or if the child is between the ages of 18 and 23 and attending school. A table on page 72 lists DIC for children.

Spina Bifida Allowance

Spina bifida patients who are children of Vietnam veterans are eligible for vocational training, health care, and a monthly allowance. Contact a VA regional office to apply for medical treatment or benefits payments. The monthly allowance is set at three levels, depending upon the degree of disability suffered by the child. The three levels are based on neurological manifestations that define the severity of disability: impairment of the functioning of the extremities, impairment of bowel or bladder function, and impairment of intellectual functioning. Allowances for 2000 are listed on page 73.

Special Allowances

Surviving spouses and parents receiving DIC may be granted a special allowance to pay for aid and attendance by another person if they are patients in a nursing home or require the regular assistance of another person. Surviving spouses receiving DIC may be granted a housebound special allowance if they are permanently housebound. A table on page 72 lists the amount of the current allowances for spouses.

Restored Entitlement Program for Survivors

Survivors of veterans who died of service-connected causes incurred or aggravated prior to Aug. 13, 1981, may be eligible for special benefits. This benefit is similar to the benefits for students and surviving spouses with children between ages 16 and 18 that were eliminated from Social Security benefits. The benefits are payable in addition to any other benefits to which the family may be entitled. The amount of the benefit is based on information provided by the Social Security Administration.

Death Pension

Pensions based on need are available for surviving spouses and unmarried children of deceased veterans with wartime service.

Spouses must not have remarried and children must be under age 18, or under age 23 if attending a VA-approved school. Pension is not payable to those with estates large enough to provide maintenance. The veteran must have been discharged under conditions other than dishonorable and must have had 90 days or more of active military service, at least one day of which was during a period of war, or a service-connected disability justifying discharge for disability. If the veteran died in service but not in line of duty, benefits may be payable if the veteran had completed at least two years of honorable service. Children who became incapable of self-support because of a disability before age 18 may be eligible for a pension as long as the condition exists, unless the child marries or the child's income exceeds the applicable limit. A surviving spouse may be entitled to higher income limitations or additional benefits if living in a nursing home, in need of aid and attendance by another person or permanently housebound.

The Improved Pension program provides a monthly payment to bring an eligible person's income to a support level established by law. The payment is reduced by the annual income from other sources such as Social Security paid to the surviving spouse or dependent children. Medical expenses may be deducted from the income ceiling. Pension is not payable to those who have assets that can be used to provide adequate maintenance. Maximum rates for the Improved Death Pension are listed on page 70.

Dependents' Education

Educational assistance benefits are available to spouses who have not remarried and children of: (1) veterans who died or are permanently and totally disabled as the result of a disability arising from active military service; (2) veterans who died from any cause while rated permanently and totally disabled from service-connected disability; (3) servicemembers listed for more than 90 days as currently missing in action or captured in line of duty by a hostile force; (4) servicemembers listed for more than 90 days as currently detained or interned by a foreign government or power.

The termination of a surviving spouse's remarriage — by death, divorce, or ceasing to live with another person as that person's spouse — will reinstate Dependents' Educational Assistance benefits to the surviving spouse.

Benefits may be awarded for pursuit of associate, bachelor or graduate degrees at colleges and universities — including independent study, cooperative training and study abroad programs. Courses leading to a certificate or diploma from business, technical or vocational schools also may be taken.

Benefits may be awarded for apprenticeships, on-job training programs and farm cooperative courses. Benefits for correspondence courses under certain conditions are available to spouses only. Secondary-school programs may be pursued if the individual is not a high-school graduate. An individual with a deficiency in a subject may receive tutorial assistance benefits if enrolled halftime or more. Deficiency, refresher and other training also may be available.

Monthly Payments. Payments are made monthly. The rate is $485 a month for full-time school attendance, with lesser amounts for part-time training. A person may receive educational assistance for full-time training for up to 45 months or the equivalent in part-time training. Payments to a spouse end 10 years from the date the individual is found eligible or from the date of the death of the veteran. VA may grant an extension. Children generally must be between the ages of 18 and 26 to receive education benefits, though extensions may be granted.

Work-Study. Participants must train at the three-quarter or full-time rate. They may be paid in advance 40 percent of the amount specified in the work-study agreement or an amount equal to 50 times the applicable minimum wage, whichever is less. Participants under the supervision of a VA employee may provide outreach services, prepare and process VA paperwork, and work at a VA medical facility or perform other approved activities.

Counseling Services. VA may provide counseling services to help an eligible dependent pursue an educational or vocational objective.

Special Benefits. An eligible child over age 14 with a physical or mental disability that impairs pursuit of an educational program may receive special restorative training to lessen or overcome that impairment. This training may include speech and voice correction, language retraining, lip reading, auditory training, Braille reading and writing, and similar programs. Specialized vocational training also is available to an eligible spouse or child over age 14 who is handicapped by a physical or mental disability that prevents pursuit of an educational program.

Spina Bifida Assistance. A child with spina bifida, who is parented by a Vietnam veteran, can receive vocational training to guide the child, parent or guardian in choosing a vocational training program. VA also will provide up to 24 months of training to achieve a vocational goal.

Educational Loans

Loans are available to spouses who qualify for educational assistance. Spouses who have passed their 10-year period of eligibility may be eligible for an educational loan. During the first two years after the end of their eligibility period, they may borrow up to $2,500 per academic year to continue a full-time course leading to a college degree or to a professional or vocational objective which requires at least six months to complete. VA may waive the six-month requirement. Loans are based on financial need.

Home Loan Guaranties

A VA loan guaranty to acquire a home may be available to an unremarried spouse of a veteran or servicemember who died as a result of service-connected disabilities, or to a spouse of a servicemember who has been officially listed as missing in action or as a prisoner of war for more than 90 days. Spouses of those listed as prisoners of war or missing in action are limited to one loan.

Montgomery GI Bill Death Benefit

VA will pay a special Montgomery GI Bill death benefit to a designated survivor in the event of the service-connected death of an individual while on active duty or within one year after discharge or release. The deceased must either have been entitled to educational assistance under the Montgomery GI Bill program or a participant in the program who would have been so entitled but for the high school diploma or length-of-service requirement. The amount paid will be equal to the participant's actual military pay reduction less any education benefits paid.

Women Veterans

Women veterans are eligible for the same VA benefits as male veterans. Additional services and benefits for women veterans are gender-specific, and include breast and pelvic examinations and other general reproductive health-care services. Preventive health care provided includes counseling, contraceptive services, menopause management, Pap smears and mammography. Referrals are made for services that VA is unable to provide.

VA health-care professionals provide counseling and treatment to help veterans overcome psychological trauma resulting from sexual trauma during active military service. Appropriate care and services are provided for any injury, illness or psychological condition resulting from such trauma.

To ensure privacy for women veterans, VA medical centers have made structural changes. Women Veterans' Coordinators are available at all VA facilities to assist women veterans seeking treatment and benefits.

Homeless Veterans

A number of VA benefits prevent at-risk veterans from becoming homeless, including disability compensation, pension and education benefits. VA conducts community-based "stand downs" to make benefits information and assistance more accessible to homeless veterans. Homeless veterans also are provided special assistance through many other VA program initiatives.

In addition, VA provides health and rehabilitation programs for homeless veterans. Health Care for Homeless Veterans programs provide outreach and comprehensive medical, psychological and rehabilitation treatment programs. Domiciliary Care for Homeless Veterans programs provide residential rehabilitation services. VA has a growing number of Compensated Work Therapy/Therapeutic Residence group homes, special daytime, drop-in centers, and Comprehensive Homeless Centers.

VA's Homeless Providers Grant and Per Diem Program assists nonprofit and local government agencies to establish housing or service centers for homeless veterans. Grants are awarded for the construction, acquisition or renovation of facilities. VA also has joined with the Department of Housing and Urban Development, the Social Security Administration, veterans service organizations, and community nonprofit groups to assist homeless veterans. For information on benefits for homeless veterans, contact the nearest VA facility.

Overseas Benefits

Medical Benefits

VA will pay for medical services for the treatment of service-connected disabilities and related conditions for veterans abroad. VA does not authorize nursing-home care in foreign jurisdictions, except for the Philippines. Services in most foreign countries must be authorized by the Foreign Medical Program Office, PO Box 65021, Denver, CO 80206-9021, USA, phone 303-331-7590. Services provided in Canada are under the jurisdiction of the VA Center in White River Junction, VT 05009-0001, USA, phone 802-296-6379. Services provided in the Philippines are under the jurisdiction of the U.S. VA office in Pasay City, phone 011-632-833-4566.

Other Overseas Benefits

VA monetary benefits, including compensation, pension, educational assistance and burial allowances, generally are payable overseas. Some programs in foreign jurisdictions are restricted. Home-loan guaranties are available only in the United States and selected U.S. territories and possessions. Educational benefits are limited to approved degree-granting programs in institutions of higher learning. Beneficiaries residing in foreign countries should contact the nearest American embassy or consulate for information and claims assistance. In Canada, veterans should contact an office of Veterans Affairs Canada.

Benefits for Special Groups

A number of groups who have provided military-related service to the United States have been granted VA benefits. For the service to qualify, the Defense Secretary must certify that the group has provided active military service. Individual members must be issued a discharge by the Defense Secretary to qualify for VA benefits. Service in the following groups has been certified as active military service for benefits purposes:

1. Women Airforce Service Pilots (WASPs).
2. World War I Signal Corps Female Telephone Operators Unit.
3. Engineer Field Clerks.
4. Women's Army Auxiliary Corps (WAAC).
5. Quartermaster Corps female clerical employees serving with the American Expeditionary Forces in World War I.

6. Civilian employees of Pacific naval air bases who actively participated in defense of Wake Island during World War II.

7. Reconstruction aides and dietitians in World War I.

8. Male civilian ferry pilots.

9. Wake Island defenders from Guam.

10. Civilian personnel assigned to OSS secret intelligence.

11. Guam Combat Patrol.

12. Quartermaster Corps members of the Keswick crew on Corregidor during World War II.

13. U.S. civilians who participated in the defense of Bataan.

14. U.S. merchant seamen who served on blockships in support of Operation Mulberry in the World War II invasion of Normandy.

15. American merchant marines in oceangoing service during World War II.

16. Civilian Navy IFF radar technicians who served in combat areas of the Pacific during World War II.

17. U.S. civilians of the American Field Service who served overseas in World War I.

18. U.S. civilians of the American Field Service who served overseas under U.S. armies and U.S. army groups in World War II.

19. U.S. civilian employees of American Airlines who served overseas in a contract with the Air Transport Command between Dec. 14, 1941, and Aug. 14, 1945.

20. Civilian crewmen of U.S. Coast and Geodetic Survey vessels who served in areas of immediate military hazard while conducting cooperative operations with and for the U.S. Armed Forces between Dec. 7, 1941, and Aug. 15, 1945.

21. Members of the American Volunteer Group (Flying Tigers) who served between Dec. 7, 1941, and July 18, 1942.

22. U.S. civilian flight crew and aviation ground support employees of United Air Lines who served overseas in a contract with Air Transport Command between Dec. 14, 1941, and Aug. 14, 1945.

23. U.S. civilian flight crew and aviation ground support employees of Transcontinental and Western Air, Inc. (TWA), who served overseas in a contract with the Air Transport Command between Dec. 14, 1941, and Aug. 14, 1945.

24. U.S. civilian flight crew and aviation ground support employees of Consolidated Vultee Aircraft Corp. (Consairway Division) who served overseas in a contract with Air Transport Command between Dec. 14, 1941, and Aug. 14, 1945.

25. U.S. civilian flight crew and aviation ground support employees of Pan American World Airways and its subsidiaries and affiliates, who served overseas in a contract with the Air Transport

Command and Naval Air Transport Service between Dec. 14, 1941, and Aug. 14, 1945.

26. Honorably discharged members of the American Volunteer Guard, Eritrea Service Command, between June 21, 1942, and March 31, 1943.

27. U.S. civilian flight crew and aviation ground support employees of Northwest Airlines who served overseas under the airline's contract with Air Transport Command from Dec. 14, 1941, through Aug. 14, 1945.

28. U.S. civilian female employees of the U.S. Army Nurse Corps who served in the defense of Bataan and Corregidor during the period January 2, 1942, to February 3, 1945.

29. U.S. flight crew and aviation ground support employees of Northeast Airlines Atlantic Division, who served overseas as a result of Northeast Airlines' contract with the Air Transport Command during the period December 7, 1941, through August 14, 1945.

30. U.S. civilian flight crew and aviation ground support employees of Braniff Airways, who served overseas in the North Atlantic or under the jurisdiction of the North Atlantic Wing, Air Transport Command, as a result of a contract with the Air Transport Command during the period February 26, 1942, through August 14, 1945.

Small and Disadvantaged
Business Utilization

The Office of Small and Disadvantaged Business Utilization helps small businesses obtain information on acquiring contracts with VA. Like other federal offices, VA is required to place a portion of its contracts and purchases with small and disadvantaged businesses. VA contracting offices are encouraged to include veteran-owned contractors in bid solicitations and to meet government-wide goals for utilizing businesses owned by service-disabled veterans. Information on these businesses can be found under "Procurement PRO-Net" on the Small Business Administration's World Wide Web page (http://www.sba.gov/VETS). For more information, write to OSDBU (00SB), Department of Veterans Affairs, 810 Vermont Ave., N.W., Washington, DC 20420, or connect to the OSDBU web page (http://www.va.gov/OSDBU).

OTHER FEDERAL BENEFITS

Some benefits for veterans and their dependents are not administered by the Department of Veterans Affairs. The following information describes these benefits and how to apply for them.

Job-Finding Assistance

State employment service offices help veterans find jobs by providing free job counseling, testing, referral and placement services. Veterans are given priority in referral for job openings and training opportunities. Disabled veterans receive the highest priority in referrals. Employment offices also assist veterans by providing information about unemployment compensation, job markets and on-the-job and apprenticeship training opportunities. Veterans should present a copy of their military discharge, form DD-214, at the nearest state employment service office.

Job Partnership Training Act

The Job Partnership Training Act provides for a national job training program for disabled, Vietnam Era and recently separated veterans. Job training programs may be conducted through public agencies and private nonprofit organizations. Veterans should apply at the nearest state employment service office.

Disabled Veterans Outreach Program

The Disabled Veterans Outreach Program locates disabled veterans and helps them find jobs. Outreach staff members, many of whom are disabled veterans themselves, are located in state employment service offices and One-Stop centers, but some may be stationed in VA regional offices and readjustment counseling centers (VET Centers).

Re-employment Rights

A person who left a civilian job to enter active duty in the Armed Forces may be entitled to return to the job after discharge or release from active duty. Re-employment rights are provided for those who served in the active duty or reserve components of the Armed

Forces. To be re-employed, four requirements must be met: (1) the person must give advance notice of military service to the employer; (2) the cumulative absence from the civilian job shall not exceed five years (with some exceptions); (3) the person must submit a timely application for re-employment; and (4) the person must not have been released with a dishonorable or other punitive discharge.

The law calls for the returning veteran to be placed in the job as if the veteran had remained continuously employed. This means that the person may be entitled to benefits that are based on seniority, such as pensions, pay increases and promotions. The law also prohibits discrimination in hiring, promotion or other advantages of employment on the basis of military service.

Applications for re-employment should be given, verbally or in writing, to a person authorized to represent the company for hiring purposes. A record should be kept of the application. If there are problems in attaining re-employment, the employee should contact the Department of Labor's Veterans' Employment and Training Service (VETS) in the state of the employer concerned. This applies to private sector, as well as state, local and federal government employees, including the Postal Service.

Employees should contact their agency personnel office about restoring rights. If a job is not restored or is restored improperly, the employee has the right to file a complaint with VETS. Additionally, a federal employee may appeal directly to the Merit Systems Protection Board. Non-federal employees may file a complaint in U.S. district court. Information is available on the Internet through VETS' USERRA Advisor Expert System (http://www.dol.gov/dol/vets).

Unemployment Compensation

Weekly unemployment compensation may be paid to discharged servicemembers for a limited period of time. The amount and duration of payments are governed by state laws. To apply, veterans should immediately contact their nearest state employment office after leaving military service and present a copy of their military discharge, form DD-214.

Federal Contractor Affirmative Action

Federal legislation prohibits employers with federal contracts from discriminating in employment against individuals who served on active duty during a war or in a campaign or expedition for which a campaign badge has been authorized, Vietnam-Era veterans who served on active duty for more than 180 days, any part of which occurred during the period listed on page 10 and who were discharged or released with other than a dishonorable discharge or who were discharged or released with a service-connected disability. Federal legislation also prohibits employers with federal contracts from discriminating in employment against "special disabled" veterans. Special disabled veterans are veterans who have a VA disability rating of 30 percent or more, veterans who are rated at 10 or 20 percent who have been determined to have a serious employment handicap and veterans who were discharged or released from active duty because of a service-connected disability. Federal legislation requires these contractors to take affirmative action to employ and advance in employment campaign veterans, Vietnam-Era and special disabled veterans. It also requires these contractors to list jobs with offices of the state employment service, including full-time employment, temporary employment and part-time employment. Veterans who believe their rights have been violated may file a complaint with the U.S. Department of Labor or at a state employment office.

Federal Jobs for Veterans

The Veterans Readjustment Appointment (VRA) authority provides veterans with jobs in the federal government. The VRA authority allows federal agencies to appoint Vietnam-Era and post-Vietnam-Era veterans to jobs without competition. Such appointments may lead to conversion to career or career-conditional employment upon satisfactory work for two years. Veterans seeking VRA appointment should apply directly to the agency where they wish to work.

The Office of Personnel Management administers the Disabled Veterans Affirmative Action Program (DVAAP). All federal departments and agencies are required to establish plans to facilitate the recruitment and advancement of disabled veterans.

Veterans who are disabled or who served during certain periods have preference in federal jobs. This preference includes additional points to passing scores in examinations, first consideration for certain jobs, and preference in job retention. Preference also is provided for unremarried widows and widowers of deceased veterans and mothers of military personnel who died in service; spouses of service-connected disabled veterans who are no longer able to work in their usual occupations; and mothers of veterans who have permanent and total service-connected disabilities. Individuals interested in federal employment should contact the personnel offices of the federal agencies in which they wish to be employed. Information also may be obtained by contacting any Office of Personnel Management service center. The centers are listed in telephone books under U.S. Government. Information regarding job opportunities is provided by Career America Connection at 912-757-3000, as well as a convenient computer home page (http://www.usajobs.opm.gov).

Transition Assistance Program

The Transition Assistance Program assists servicemembers and their spouses who are scheduled for separation from active duty. The program, a joint effort by the Department of Defense, Department of Labor, Department of Transportation and VA, provides employment and training information to servicemembers within 180 days of their separation from the military. Three-day workshops to help veterans and their spouses make the transition from military to civilian employment are conducted at military installations. Additional counseling is available to disabled servicemembers. For more information, contact the nearest state employment service office or the Transition Office on the nearest military base.

Operation Transition

The military services provide civilian-transition counseling at least 90 days prior to each servicemember's discharge in a program called Operation Transition. A Defense Department document (DD Form 2586) is prepared that provides military experience, training history, civilian job equivalent experience and recommended educational credit. The document is delivered to servicemembers 90 to 180 days before the scheduled separation.

The Defense Outplacement Referral System (DORS) refers resumes to potential employers through 350 Transition offices worldwide. Resumes are provided to employers by mail, electronic mail, or facsimile. Employers may place job ads on the electronic Transition Bulletin Board (TBB) kept by Transition offices. Those employers having the proper computer equipment are able to place their ads electronically; others may mail or fax their ads to the TBB. Servicemembers are encouraged to respond directly to employers with their resumes. The electronic bulletin board also contains business opportunities, a calendar of transition seminars and events, and other helpful information.

Two special registries have been developed at Transition offices to help separating servicemembers obtain public community service jobs. The "Registry of Public and Community Service Organizations" contains information on organizations desiring to hire servicemembers. The "Personnel Registry" lists servicemembers who desire employment in public and community service occupations. The Defense Department matches people and employers on the two registries, and counsels separating servicemembers on how to apply for positions with public and community service organizations.

Loans for Farms and Homes

Loans and guaranties may be provided by the U.S. Department of Agriculture to buy, improve or operate farms. Loans and guaranties are available for housing in towns generally up to 20,000 in population. Applications from veterans have preference. For further information contact Farm Service Agency or Rural Economic and Community Development, U.S. Department of Agriculture, Washington, DC 20250, or apply at local Department of Agriculture offices, usually located in county seats.

FHA Home Mortgage Insurance

The Federal Housing Administration is responsible for the Home Mortgage Insurance Program for Veterans. These home loans can require less down payment than other FHA programs. Veterans on active duty are eligible if they enlisted before Sept. 8, 1980, or entered on active duty before Oct. 14, 1982, and were discharged under other than dishonorable conditions with at least 90 days service. Veterans with enlisted service after Sept. 7, 1980, or who entered on active duty after Oct. 16, 1981, must have served at least 24 months unless discharged for hardship or disability. Active duty for training is qualifying service. Submit VA Form 26-8261a to VA for a Certificate of Veteran Status. This certificate is submitted by the lender to FHA.

Naturalization Preference

Aliens with honorable service in the U.S. Armed Forces during hostilities may be naturalized without having to comply with the general requirements for naturalization. Such aliens must have been lawfully admitted to the United States for permanent residence or have been inducted, enlisted, re-enlisted or extended an enlistment in the Armed Forces while within the United States, Puerto Rico, Guam, the Virgin Islands of the United States, the Canal Zone, American Samoa, Northern Marianas or Swain's Island. Hostilities must be periods declared by the President. Aliens with honorable service in the U.S. Armed Forces for three years or more during periods not considered a conflict or hostility by Executive Order may be naturalized provided they have been lawfully admitted to the United States for permanent residence. Applications must be made while on active duty or within six months of discharge.

Aliens who have served honorably after Oct. 15, 1978, for at least 12 years may be granted special immigrant status. Aliens who died as a result of wounds incurred or disease contracted during periods of hostilities declared by the President may receive recognition as U.S. citizens. An application may be submitted by the person's next of kin or other authorized representative. This posthumous citizenship is honorary only and does not confer any other benefits to the person's surviving relatives. For assistance, contact the nearest office of the Immigration and Naturalization Service, Justice Department.

Small Business Administration

A number of SBA programs are designed to help small businesses, including businesses owned or operated by veterans. Help available from the SBA includes business training, conferences, counseling, surety bonding, government procurement and financial management assistance. Loans from the SBA are made under its Loan Guaranty Program. The loan amount is advanced by the bank or other lending institution, with SBA guaranteeing up to 85 percent of the total amount. Each SBA field office designates a veterans affairs officer to assist veterans. Information about SBA's programs is provided at field offices. Check the local phone book for the nearest SBA office or call 1-800-827-5722. Information is also available on the SBA website (http://www.sba.gov).

Social Security

Monthly retirement, disability and survivor benefits under Social Security are payable to a veteran and dependents if the veteran has earned enough work credits under the program. Upon the veteran's death, a one-time payment of $255 also may be made to the veteran's spouse or child. In addition, a veteran may qualify at age 65 for Medicare's hospital insurance and medical insurance. Medicare protection also is available to people who have received Social Security disability benefits for 24 months, and to insured people and their dependents who need dialysis or kidney transplants.

Active duty or active duty for training in the U.S. uniformed services has counted toward Social Security since January 1957. Since Jan. 1,

1988, work as a member of the Armed Forces Reserve components while on inactive duty for training also counts toward Social Security. Servicemembers and veterans receive an extra $300 credit for each quarter in which they received any basic pay for active duty or active duty for training after 1956 and before 1978. After 1977, a credit of $100 is granted for each $300 of reported wages up to a maximum credit of $1,200. No additional Social Security taxes are withheld from pay for these extra credits. Also, noncontributory Social Security credits of $160 a month may be granted to veterans who served after Sept. 15, 1940, and before 1957, including attendance at service academies. Further information about Social Security credits and benefits is available from Social Security offices or by calling 1-800-772-1213.

Supplemental Security Income

For those age 65 or older and those who are blind or otherwise disabled, Supplemental Security Income (SSI) may be provided, if they have little or no income or resources. States may supplement the federal payments to eligible persons and may disregard additional income. Although VA compensation and pension benefits are counted in determining income for SSI purposes, some income is not counted. Also, not all resources count in determining eligibility. For example, a person's home and the land it is on do not count. Personal effects, household goods, automobiles and life insurance may not count, depending upon their value. Information and assistance in applying for these payments may be obtained at any Social Security office or by calling 1-800-772-1213.

Passports to Visit Overseas Cemeteries

"No-fee" passports are available for family members visiting overseas graves and memorial sites of World War I and World War II dead. Those eligible for such passports include surviving spouses, parents, children, sisters, brothers and guardians of the deceased who are buried or commemorated in American military cemeteries on foreign soil. For additional information, write to the American Battle Monuments Commission, Courthouse Plaza II, Suite 500, 2300 Clarendon Blvd., Arlington, VA 22201, or phone 703-696-6897.

Medals

Medals awarded while in active service are issued by the appropriate service if requested by veterans or, if deceased, their next of kin. Requests for medals from the Navy, Marine Corps and Coast Guard should be sent to the U.S. Navy Liaison Office, National Personnel

Records Center, Room 3475, 9700 Page Blvd., St. Louis, MO 63132-5100. Requests for medals from the Army should be sent to the U.S. Army Reserve Personnel Center, ATTN: ARPC-VSE, 9700 Page Blvd., St. Louis, MO 63132-5100. Requests for medals from the Air Force should be sent to the National Personnel Records Center (Military Personnel Records), 9700 Page Blvd., St. Louis, MO 63132-5100. The veteran's full name should be printed or typed, so that it can be read clearly. The request must contain the signature of the veteran or the signature of the next of kin if the veteran is deceased. Include the veteran's branch of service, service number or Social Security number and exact or approximate dates of service. If available, include a copy of the discharge or separation document, WDAGO Form 53-55 or DD Form 214. If possible, send the request on Standard Form 180, "Request Pertaining To Military Records." These forms are available from VA offices or veterans organizations.

Review of Discharges

Each of the military services maintains a discharge review board with authority to change, correct, or modify discharges or dismissals that are not issued by a sentence of a general court martial. The board has no authority to address medical discharges. The veteran or, if the veteran is deceased or incompetent, the surviving spouse, next of kin or legal representative may apply for a review of discharge by writing to the military department concerned, using Department of Defense Form 293. This form may be obtained at a VA office. If more than 15 years have passed since discharge, DD Form 149 should be used. Service discharge review boards conduct hearings in Washington, D.C. Traveling review boards also visit selected cities to hear cases. In addition, the Army sends teams to locations to videotape the testimony of applicants for later review by a board in Washington, D.C. Discharges awarded as a result of unauthorized absence in excess of 180 days make persons ineligible for VA benefits regardless of action taken by discharge review boards, unless VA determines there were compelling circumstances for the absences. Boards for the correction of military records also may consider such cases.

Veterans with disabilities incurred or aggravated during active military service may qualify for medical or related benefits regardless of separation and characterization of service. Veterans separated administratively under other than honorable conditions may request that their discharge be reviewed for possible recharacterization, provided they file their appeal within 15 years of the date of separation. Questions regarding the review of a discharge may be addressed to the appropriate discharge review board at the following addresses:

- Army — Army Discharge Review Board, Attention: SFMR-RBB, Room 200A, 1941 Jefferson Davis Hwy., Arlington, VA 22202-4504.
- Navy and USMC — Navy Discharge Review Board, 801 N. Randolph St., Suite 905, Arlington, VA 22203.
- Air Force — Air Force Military Personnel Center, Attention: DP-MDOA1, Randolph AFB, TX 78150-6001.
- Coast Guard — Coast Guard, Attention: GPE1, Washington, DC 20593.

Replacing Military Records

If discharge or separation papers are lost, duplicate copies may be obtained by contacting the National Personnel Records Center, Military Personnel Records, 9700 Page Blvd., St. Louis, MO 63132-5100. Specify that a duplicate separation document or discharge is needed. The veteran's full name should be printed or typed so that it can be read clearly, but the request must also contain the signature of the veteran or the signature of the next of kin, if the veteran is deceased. Include branch of service, service number or Social Security number and exact or approximate dates and years of service. Use Standard Form 180, "Request Pertaining To Military Records," available from VA offices or at the VA forms web site (http://www.va.gov/forms). It is not necessary to request a duplicate copy of a veteran's discharge or separation papers solely for the purpose of filing a claim for VA benefits. If complete information about the veteran's service is furnished on the application, VA will obtain verification of service from the National Personnel Records Center or the service department concerned. In a medical emergency, information from a veteran's records may be obtained by phoning the appropriate service: Army, 314-538-4261; Air Force, 314-538-4243; Navy, Marine Corps or Coast Guard, 314-538-4141.

Correction of Military Records

The secretary of a military department, acting through a board for correction of military records, has authority to correct any military record when necessary to correct an error or remove an injustice. Applications for correction of a military record, including review of discharges issued by courts martial, may be considered by a correction board. A request for correction generally must be filed by the veteran, survivor or legal representative within three years after discovery of the alleged error or injustice. The board may excuse failure to file within the prescribed time, however, if it finds it would be in the interest of justice to do so. It is the responsibility of the applicant to show why the filing of the application was delayed and why it would be in the interest of justice for the board to consider the application despite the delay. To justify any correction, it is necessary to show to the satisfaction of the board that the alleged entry or omission in the records was in error or unjust. Applications should include all available evidence, such as signed statements of witnesses or a brief of arguments supporting the requested correction. Application is made with DD Form 149, available at any VA office.

Armed Forces Retirement Homes

The following veterans may be eligible to live in two retirement homes run by the Armed Forces Retirement Home: veterans 60 years of age or older who have completed 20 years or more of active service; veterans incapable of earning a livelihood because of a service-connected disability incurred in the line of duty in the armed forces; other veterans incapable of earning a livelihood because of injuries, disease, or disability who served in a war theater during a time of war declared by Congress or who were eligible for hostile fire special pay; veterans who served in the women's component of the Armed Forces before the enactment of the Women's Armed Services Integration Act of 1948. Veterans are not eligible if they have been convicted of a felony or are not free from alcohol, drug or psychiatric problems.

New residents must be capable of living independently in a dormitory. The Armed Forces Retirement Home is an independent federal agency. For information, write to the Admissions Office 1094, U.S. Soldiers' and Airmen's Home, 3700 N. Capitol St. NW, Washington, DC 20317, or phone 1-800-422-9988; or write to U.S. Naval Home, 1800 Beach Drive, Gulfport, MS 39507, or phone 1-800-332-3527.

Commissary and Exchange Privileges

Unlimited exchange and commissary store privileges in the United States are available to honorably discharged veterans with a service-connected disability rated at 100 percent, unremarried surviving spouses of members or retired members of the Armed Forces, recipients of the Medal of Honor, and their dependents and orphans. Certification of total disability is done by VA. Reservists and their dependents also may be eligible. Privileges overseas are governed by international law and are available only if agreed upon by the foreign government concerned. VA provides assistance in completing DD Form 1172, "Application for Uniformed Services Identification and Privilege Card."

Death Gratuity

Military services provide a death gratuity of $6,000 to a deceased servicemember's next of kin. The death gratuity is paid for death in active service or for retirees who died within 120 days of retirement as a result of service-connected injury or illness. Parents, brothers or sisters may be provided the gratuity, if designated as next of kin by the deceased. The gratuity is paid by the last military command of the deceased. If the beneficiary is not paid automatically, application may be made to the military service concerned.

Appeals

Veterans and other claimants for VA benefits have the right to appeal decisions made by a VA regional office or medical center. Typical issues appealed are disability compensation, pension, education benefits, recovery of overpayments, medication copayment debts and reimbursement for medical services that were not authorized.

A claimant has one year from the date of the notification of a VA decision to file an appeal. The first step in the appeal process is for a claimant to file a written notice of disagreement with the VA regional office or medical center that made the decision. This is a written statement that a claimant disagrees with VA's decision. Following receipt of the written notice, VA will furnish the claimant a "Statement of the Case" describing what facts, laws and regulations were used in deciding the case. To complete the request for appeal, the claimant must file a "Substantive Appeal" within 60 days of the mailing of the Statement of the Case, or within one year from the date VA mailed its decision, whichever period ends later.

Board of Veterans' Appeals

The Board of Veterans' Appeals makes decisions on appeals on behalf of the Secretary of Veterans Affairs. Although it is not required, a claimant may be represented by a veterans service organization, an agent or an attorney. The Board reviews fee agreements between appellants and attorneys or agents. The Board also determines whether attorneys or agents are eligible for payment of fees from a claimant's past-due benefits. Appellants have the right to present their case in person to a member of the Board at a hearing in Washington, D.C., at a VA regional office or by videoconference. More information about appeals is available in the pamphlet, "Understanding the Appeal Process," which can be found on the Internet at http://www.va.gov/customer/consumer.htm. To request a copy of the pamphlet, write to the address shown below.

The text of appeal decisions may be obtained from the Internet at the website listed above or on CD-ROMs that can be purchased from the Government Printing Office or reviewed at most VA regional offices. For further information on obtaining decision CD-ROMs or requesting pamphlets, contact Department of Veterans Affairs, Board of Veterans' Appeals (01B), Washington, DC 20420.

U.S. Court of Appeals for Veterans Claims

A VA claim may be appealed from the Board of Veterans' Appeals to the U.S. Court of Appeals for Veterans Claims. This court is independent of the Department of Veterans Affairs. Only claimants may seek a review by the court; VA may not appeal board decisions.

To appeal to the court, the claimant must have filed a Notice of Disagreement on or after Nov. 18, 1988. The appeal must be filed with the court with a postmark that is within 120 days after the Board of Veterans' Appeals mails its final decision.

The court does not hold trials or receive new evidence. The court reviews the record that was considered by the Board of Veterans' Appeals. Appellants may represent themselves before the court or have lawyers or approved agents as representatives. Oral argument is held only at the direction of the court. Either party may appeal a decision of the court to the U.S. Court of Appeals for the Federal Circuit and may seek review in the Supreme Court of the United States.

The court's Internet website (http://www.vetapp.uscourts.gov) contains its decisions, case status information, rules and procedures, and other special announcements. The court's decisions can also be found on its electronic bulletin board (202-501-5836), in West's Veterans Appeals Reporter, and on the WestLaw and LEXIS on-line services. For other questions, contact the Clerk of the Court, 625 Indiana Ave. NW, Suite 900, Washington, DC 20004, or call 1-202-501-5970.

2000 Disability Compensation

Disability	Monthly Rate
10 percent	$98
20 percent	188
30 percent	288
40 percent	413
50 percent	589
60 percent	743
70 percent	937
80 percent	1,087
90 percent	1,224
100 percent	2,036

Depending upon the disability rating of the veteran, allowances for a spouse range from $35 to $117; and for each additional child, $18 to $61.

2000 Improved Pension

Status	Maximum Annual Rate
Veteran without dependent	$8,989
With one dependent	11,773
Veteran permanently housebound	10,987
With one dependent	13,771
Veteran needing regular aid and attendance	14,999
With one dependent	17,782
Two veterans married to one another	11,773
Veterans of World War I and Mexican Border Period, addition to the applicable annual rate	2,037
Increase for each additional dependent child	1,532

2000 Vocational Rehabilitation Rates
(Paid monthly ($))

Type of training*	No dependent	One dependent	Two dependents	Each add. dependent
A				
Full-time	420.45	521.54	614.60	44.80
3/4-time	315.93	391.74	459.50	34.45
1/2-time	211.39	261.91	307.87	22.98
B				
Full-time	420.45	521.54	614.60	44.80
C				
Full-time	367.62	444.57	512.35	33.32
D				
Full-time	420.45	521.54	614.60	44.80
3/4-time	315.93	391.74	459.50	34.45
1/2-time	211.39	261.91	307.87	22.98
1/4-time	105.98	130.96	153.93	11.48

*Type of training

A. Institutional or unpaid work experience in a federal, state or local agency, or a federally recognized Indian tribe agency.

B. Unpaid on-job training in a federal, state or local agency, or a federally recognized Indian tribe agency; training in a home; vocational course in a rehabilitation facility or sheltered workshop; independent instructor; institutional non-farm cooperative.

C. Farm cooperative, apprenticeship, on-job training, or on-job non-farm cooperative. The VA payment is based on the wage received.

D. Independent living or extended evaluation.

Spouses
2000 Dependency and Indemnity Compensation
(Veteran died prior to Jan. 1, 1993)

Pay Grade	Monthly Rate
E-1-E-6..................................	$881
E-7..	911
E-8..	962
E-9..	1003
W-1...	930
W-2...	968
W-3...	997
W-4...	1,054
O-1..	930
O-2..	962
O-3..	1,028
O-4..	1,087
O-5..	1,198
O-6..	1,349
O-7..	1,458
O-8..	1,598
O-9..	1,712
O-10...	1,878

Spouses
2000 Dependency and Indemnity Compensation
(Veteran died on/after Jan. 1, 1993)

Allowances	Monthly Rate
Basic Rate	$881
Additional:	
Each Dependent Child	222
Aid and Attendance	222
Housebound	107

Add $222 for each dependent child under age 18. Add $191 if veteran was totally disabled eight continuous years prior to death.

2000 Improved Death Pension

Recipient	Maximum Annual Rate ($)
Surviving spouse	6,026
With one dependent child	7,891
Surviving spouse permanently housebound	7,367
With dependent child	9,228
Surviving spouse in need of regular aid and attendance	9,635
With dependent child	11,497
Allowance for each additional dependent child	1,532
Pension for each surviving child	1,532

Spina Bifida Benefits
(Effective Dec. 1, 2000)

	Level I	Level II	Level III
Monthly Rate ($)	213	743	1,272

Provided to children of Vietnam veterans born with spina bifida. The three levels represent degree of disability.

Loan Guaranty Entitlement

Loan Amount	Guaranty Percent	Maximum Amount ($)
Up to $45,000	50	22,500
$45,001 to $56,250	40-50	22,500
$56,251 to $144,000	40	36,000
$144,001 or more	25	50,750
Manufactured home or lot	40	20,000

Funding Fees

Loan Category	Veterans % of loan	Reservists % of loan
Purchase or construction loans with down payments of less than 5 percent, refinancing loans and home improvement loans	2.0	2.75
Purchase or construction loans with down payments of at least 5 percent but less than 10 percent	1.5	2.25
Purchase or construction loans with down payments of 10 percent or more	1.25	2.0
Manufactured home loans	1.0	1.0
Interest rate reduction loans	0.5	0.5
Assumption of VA-guaranteed loans	0.5	0.5
Second or subsequent use without a down payment	3.0	3.0

Where To Find
More Information

By Phone:

For information on:	Call:
VA Benefits	1-800-827-1000
Health Benefits	1-877-222-8387
Education Benefits	1-888-442-4551
Life Insurance	1-800-669-8477
Debt Management	1-800-827-0648
Mammography Hotline	1-888-492-7844
Telecommunication Device for the Deaf (TDD)	1-800-829-4833
CHAMPVA	1-800-733-8387
Headstones and Markers	1-800-697-6947
Gulf War Helpline	1-800-749-8387

Health Eligibility Center
1644 Tullie Circle
Atlanta, GA 30329-2303

404-235-1257
or
1-800-929-8387

By Computer:

This VA Federal Benefits booklet and other VA information is available on VA's World Wide Web Home Page at:

http://www.va.gov/

VA also has a toll-free bulletin board, called VA ONLINE, which can be reached at 1-800-US1-VETS (871-8387).

VA Facilities

Note: Patients should call the telephone numbers listed to obtain clinic hours of operation and specialties served.

The following symbols indicate additional programs are available at medical centers:
* for nursing-home care units
# for domiciliaries

ALABAMA
Medical Centers:
Central AL Veterans HC System:
Montgomery 36109 (215 Perry Hill Rd., 334-272-4670
#Tuskegee 36083 (2400 Hospital Rd., 334-727-0550)
Birmingham 35233 (700 S. 19th St., 205-933-8101)
*Tuscaloosa 35404 (3701 Loop Rd. East, 205-554-2000, ext. 2228)
Clinics:
Anniston 36202 (226 E. 9th St., 256-236-1661)
Anniston 36207 (413 Quintard Ave., 256-231-7980)
Decatur 35601 (401 Lee St. N.E., AM South Bldg., Suite 606, 256-350-1531)
Dothan 36303 (1785 East Main Street, 1-800-974-6990)
Gadsden 35906 (3004 Rainbow Drive, 256-442-0766)
Gadsden 35906 (3006 Rainbow Drive, 256-413-7154)
Huntsville 35801 (201 Governor's Dr. S.W., 256-535-3101)
Huntsville 35801 (2006 Franklin St., SE, Suite 104, 256-534-1691)
Jasper 35501 (3400 Hwy 78 East, Suite 215, 205-221-7384)

Mobile 36604 (1359 Springhill Ave., 334-415-3900)
Shoals Area Sheffield 35660 (422DD Cox Blvd., 256-381-3602)
Shoals Area 35660 (422 DD Cox Blvd., 256-381-9055)
Regional Office:
Montgomery 36109 (345 Perry Hill Rd., statewide, 1-800-827-1000)
Vet Centers:
Birmingham 35233 (1500 5th Ave. S., 205-731-0550)
Mobile 36606 (2577 Govenment Blvd., 334-478-5906)
National Cemeteries:
Fort Mitchell (Seale 36875, 553 Highway 165, 334-855-4731)
Mobile 36604 (1202 Virginia Street, for information, 850-452-3357)

ALASKA
Clinic:
#Anchorage Outpatient Clinic and Regional Office 99508-2989 (2925 DeBarr Rd., 907-257-4700)
Regional Office:
Anchorage 99508-2989 (2925 DeBarr Rd., local, 257-4700; statewide, 1-800-827-1000)
Benefits Office:
Juneau 99802 (709 W. 9th St., #263, 907-586-7472)
Vet Centers:
Anchorage 99508 (4201 Tudor Centre Dr., Suite 115, 907-563-6966)
Fairbanks 99701 (542 4th Ave., Suite 100, 907-456-4238)
Kenai 99611 (445 Coral St., 907-283-5205)
Wasilla 99654 (851 E. Westpoint Ave., Suite 111, 907-376-4318)
National Cemeteries:
Fort Richardson 99505-5498 (P.O. Box 5-498, 907-384-7075)
Sitka 99835 (P.O. Box 5-498, for information, call 907-384-7075)

ARIZONA
Medical Centers:
*Phoenix 85012 (650 East Indian School Rd., 602-277-5551, Benefits 602-222-2755)
#Prescott 86313 (500 Highway 89 North, 520-445-4860)
*Tucson 85723 (3601 S. 6th Ave., 520-792-1450)
Clinics:
Kingman 86401 (1726 Beverly Ave, 520-445-4860 ext 6223)
Bellemont 86015 (Camp Navajo Army Depot, P.O. Box 16196, 520-445-4860 ext 6223)
Casa Grande 85222 (Plaza del Sol, Suites H&I, 900 E. Florence Blvd., 520-629-4900 or 1-800-470-8262)
Safford 85546 (Bureau of Land Management, 711 S. 14'th Ave., 520-629-4900 or 1-800-470-8262)
Sierra Vista 85613 (Raymond W. Bliss Army Community Health Center, Bldg. 45006, Ft. Huachuca, 520-629-4900 or 1-800-470-8262)
Yuma 85365 (2555 E. Gila Ridge Road, 520-629-4900 or 1-800-470-8262)
Mesa 85212 (6950 E. Williams Field Rd., 602-222-2630)
Show Low 85901(2450 Show Low Lake Rd., Suite 1, 520-532-1069)
Sun City 85351 (10147 Grand Ave., 602-222-2630)
Regional Office:
Phoenix 85012 (3225 N. Central Ave.; statewide, 1-800-827-1000)
Vet Centers:
Phoenix 85004 (141 E. Palm Ln., Suite 100, 602-379-4769)
Prescott 86303 (161 S. Granite St., Suite B, 520-778-3469)
Tucson 85719 (3055 N. 1st Ave., 520-882-0333)

National Cemeteries:
National Memorial Cemetery of Arizona (Phoenix 85024, 23029 N. Cave Creek Road 602-379-4615)
Prescott 86313 (500 Highway 89 N.; for information, call 602-379-4615)

ARKANSAS
Medical Centers:
Fayetteville 72703 (1100 N. College Ave., 501-443-4301)
#*Little Rock 72205 (4300 W. 7th St., 501-257-1000)
Clinic:
Paragould 72450 (1101 West Morgan, Suite #8, 870-236-9756)
Regional Office:
North Little Rock 72115 (Bldg. 65, Ft. Roots, P.O. Box 1280; statewide, 1-800-827-1000)
Vet Center:
North Little Rock 72114 (201 W. Broadway, Suite A, 501-324-6395)
National Cemeteries:
Fayetteville 72701 (700 Government Avenue, 501-444-5051)
Fort Smith 72901 (522 Garland Ave. 501-783-5345)
Little Rock 72206 (2523 Confederate Boulevard, 501-324-6401)

CALIFORNIA
Medical Centers:
*Fresno 93703 (2615 E. Clinton Ave., 559-225-6100)
Greater Los Angeles HC System:
*Bakersfield 93301(1801 Westwind Drive 661-632-1892)
*Los Angeles 90012 (351 E. Temple St., 213-253-2677)
*Sepulveda 91343 (16111 Plummer St., 818-891-7711)
*Santa Barbara 93110 (4440 Calle Real, 805-683-1491)
*West Los Angeles 90073 (11301 Wilshire Blvd., 310-478-3711)

*Loma Linda 92357 (11201 Benton St., 909-825-7084 or 1-800-741-8387)

*Long Beach 90822 (5901 E. 7th St., 562-494-2611)

Northern Calif. HC System:
*Martinez 94553 (150 Muir Rd., 925-372-2000)

Palo Alto HC System:
#*Palo Alto 94304 (3801 Miranda Ave., 650-493-5000)
*Livermore 94550 (4951 Arroyo Rd., 925-447-2560)

*San Diego 92161 (3350 La Jolla Village Dr., 858-552-7427)

*San Francisco 94121 (4150 Clement St., 415-221-4810)

Clinics:

Atwater 95301 (3605 Hospital Road, Suite D, 209—381-0105)

Auburn 95603 (3123 Professional Drive, 1-888-227-5404)

Bakersfield 93301 (1801 Westwind Dr., 661-632-1800)

Capitola 95010 (co-located at Santa Cruz Co. Vet Center, 1350 N. 41st St., Suite 102, 831-464-5519)

Chico 95928 (25 Main Street, Suite 101, 530-879-5000

Commerce 90040 (5400 E. Olympic Blvd., Suite 150, 213-725-7557)

Eureka 95501 (727 E. Street, 707-433-6086)

Fairfield 94535 (101 Bodin Circle, Travis AFB, 707-437-7418)

*Martinez 94553 (150 Muir Road, 925-372-2000)

Modesto 95350 (826 Scenic Dr, 209-558-7300)

Monterey 93955 (located at Fort Ord, 3401 Engineer Lane, Seaside, 831-883-3800)

Oakland OPC 94612 (2221 Martin Luther King Jr. Way, 510-267-7820)

Oakland MHC 94626 (Oakland Army Base, Bldg 762, 510-587-3400)

Palm Desert 92211 (41865 Boardwalk, Suite 103, 760-341-5570 or 800-741-8387

Redding OPC 96002 (351 Hartnell Ave., 530-226-7509)

Sacramento Medical Center 95655 (10535 Hospital Way, 916-366-5366)

Sacramento MHC 95655 (10633 Grissom Ave., 916-366-5428)

San Diego 92108 (8810 Rio San Diego Dr., 619-400-5000)

San Francisco (13th & Mission) 94103 (205 13th Street, 415-551-7300)

San Jose 95119 (80 Great Oaks, 408-363-3000)

Santa Barbara 93110 (4440 Calle Real, 805-683-1491)

Santa Rosa 95403 (3315 Chanate Rd., 707-570-3800)

Seaside 93955 (3401 Engineer Ln., 831-883-3800)

Stockton 95231 (co-located with San Joaquin General Hospital, 500 Hospital Rd., 209-468-7040)

Sun City 92585 (27990 Sherman Rd., 909-672-1931 or 800-741-8387)

Tulare 93274 (850 Gem Street, 559-684-8703)

Vallejo OPC 94592 (Bldg. 201, Walnut Avenue, 707-562-8200)

Victorville 92392 (12138 Industrial St., Suite 120, 760-951-2599 or 800-741-8387)

Regional Offices:

Los Angeles 90024 (Fed. Bldg., 11000 Wilshire Blvd., serving counties of Inyo, Kern, Los Angeles, Orange, San Bernardino, San Luis Obispo, Santa Barbara and Ventura; statewide, 1-800-827-1000)

San Diego 92108 (8810 Rio San Diego Dr., serving counties of Imperial, Riverside and San Diego; statewide,1-800-827-1000)

Oakland 94612 (1301 Clay St., Rm. 1300 North; statewide, 1-800-827-1000)
(Recorded benefits, 24-hour availability, 510-637-1325)
Counties of Alpine, Lassen, Modoc and Mono served by RO in Reno, Nev.

Benefits Office:
Commerce 90022 (5400 E. Olympic Blvd., 310-235-6199)

Vet Centers:
Anaheim 92805 (859 S. Harbor Blvd., 714-776-0161)
Chico 95928 (25 Main St., 530-899-8549)
Chula Vista 91910 (835 Third Ave., 619- 409-1600)
Commerce 90022 (5400 E. Olympic Blvd., #140, 323-728-9966)
Concord 94520 (1899 Clayton Rd., Suite 140, 925-680-4526)
Eureka 95501 (2830 G St., Suite A, 707-444-8271)
Fresno 93726 (3636 N. 1st St., Suite 112, 559-487-5660)
Los Angeles 90247 (1045 W. Redondo Beach Blvd., Gardena, 310-767-1221)
Los Angeles 90230 (5730 Uplander Way, Culver City, 310-641-0326)
Marina 93933 (455 Reservation Rd., Suite E, 408-384-1660)
Oakland 94612 (1504 Franklin St., #200, 510-763-3904)
Redwood City 94062 (2946 Broadway St., 415-299-0672)
Riverside 92504 (4954 Arlington Ave., Suite A, 909-359-8967)
Rohnert Park 94928 (6225 State Farm Dr., Suite 101, 707-586-3295)
Sacramento 95825 (1111 Howe Ave., Suite 390, 916-566-7430)
San Diego 92103 (2900 6th Ave., 619-294-2040)
San Francisco 94103 (205 13th St., Suite 3190, 415-431-6021)

San Jose 95112 (278 N. 2nd St., 408-993-0729)
San Bernardino 92408 (155 West Hospitality Lane, Suite #140, 909-890-0797)
Santa Barbara 93101 (1300 Santa Barbara St., 805-564-2345)
Sepulveda 91343 (9737 Hascle St., 818-892-9227)
Upland 91786 (313 N. Mountain Ave., 909-982-0416)
Vista 92083 (1830 West Dr., Suite 103, 858-945-8941)

National Cemeteries:
Fort Rosecrans 92106 (P.O. Box 6237 Point Loma, San Diego, 619-553-2084)
Golden Gate 94066 (1300 Sneath Lane, San Bruno, 650-761-1646)
Los Angeles 90049 (950 South Sepulveda Blvd., 310-268-4675)
Riverside 92518 (22495 Van Buren Blvd., 909-653-8417)
San Francisco 94129 (P.O. Box 29012, Presidio of San Francisco, 650-761-1646)
San Joaquin Valley 95322 (32053 West McCabe Road, Gustine, 209-854-1040)

COLORADO
Medical Centers:
*Denver 80220 (1055 Clermont St., 303-399-8020)
*Southern Colorado HC System Fort Lyon 81038 (C St., 719-384-3100)
*Grand Junction 81501 (2121 North Ave., 970-242-0731)

Clinics:
Aurora 80045 (12101 E. Colfax Ave., Bldg. 500, 303-724-0190)
Colorado Springs 80905 (25 N. Spruce St., 719-380-0004)
Greeley 80631 (2020 16th Street, 970-313-0027)
Montrose 81401 (4 Hillcrest Plaza Way, 970-249-7791)

80

Sidney 69162 (645 Osage Street,
308-254-5825
Regional Office:
Denver 80225 (155 Van Gordon St.;
statewide, 1-800-827-1000)
Vet Centers:
Boulder 80302 (2128 Pearl St., 303-
440-7306)
Colorado Springs 80903 (416 E.
Colorado Ave., 719-471-9992)
Denver 80220 (7465 E. Academy
Blvd., 303-326-0645)
National Cemeteries:
Fort Logan 80235 (3698 S.
Sheridan Boulevard., Denver,
303-761-0117)
Fort Lyon 81038 (VA Medical
Center, 303-761-0117)

CONNECTICUT
Medical Centers:
Conn. HC System:
*West Haven Division 06516 (950
Campbell Ave., 203-932-5711)
Newington Division 06111 (555
Willard Ave., 860-666-6951)
Clinics:
Stamford 06904 (128 Strawberry Hill
Avenue, 1-888-844-4441)
New London 06320 (15 Mohegan
Avenue, 860-437-3611)
Waterbury 06706 (133 Scovill Street;
203-465-5292)
Windham 06226 (96 Mansfield
Street, 860-450-7583)
Winsted 06098 (115 Spencer
Street, 860-738-6985)
Regional Office:
Hartford 06103 (450 Main St.;
statewide, 1-800-827-1000)
Vet Centers:
Hartford 06120 (380 Market St.,
860-240-3543)
New Haven 06516 (141 Captain
Thomas Blvd., 203-932-9899)
Norwich 06360 (60 Main St., 860-
887-1755)

DELAWARE
Medical Center:
*Wilmington 19805 (1601 Kirkwood
Highway, 302-994-2511)
Clinic:
Millsboro 19966 (214 W. DuPont
Highway, 302-633-5212)
Regional Office:
Wilmington 19805 (1601 Kirkwood
Hwy.; statewide, 1-800-827-1000)
Vet Center:
Wilmington 19805 (VAMROC Bldg.
2, 1601 Kirkwood Highway, 302-
994-1660)

DISTRICT OF COLUMBIA:
Medical Center:
*Washington, D.C. 20422 (50 Irving
St., N.W., 202-745-8000)
Regional Office:
Washington, D.C. 20421 (1120
Vermont Ave., N.W., local, 1-800-
827-1000)
Vet Center:
Washington, D.C. 20002 (911 2nd
St., N.E., 202-543-8821)

FLORIDA
Medical Centers:
#*Bay Pines 33708 (10000 Bay
Pines Blvd., N., 727-398-6661)
N. Florida/S. Georgia HC System:
*Gainesville 32608 (1601 South-
west Archer Rd., 352-379-4095)
*Lake City 32025 (801 S. Marion
St., 904-755-3016, ext. 2463)
*Miami 33125 (1201 N.W. 16th St.,
305-324-3122)
*Tampa 33612 (13000 Bruce B.
Downs Blvd., 813-972-7604)
*West Palm Beach 33410 (7305 N.
Military Trail, 561-882-6888)
Clinics:
Bartow 33830 (1255 Brice Blvd.,
941-533-6410)
Brevard 32949 (2900 Veterans Way,
Viera, 407-637-3788)

Brooksville 34613 (14540 Cortez
Blvd., Suite 202, 352-597-8287)
Daytona Beach 32117 (1900 Mason
Ave., 904-274-4600)
Fort Myers 33916 (3033 Winkler
Extension, 941-939-3939)
Ft. Pierce 34950 (728 North US 1,
561-595-5150)
Homestead 33030 (1036 NW 1st
Avenue, 305-248-1036)
Jacksonville 32206 (1833 Boule-
vard, 904-232-2712)
Key Largo 33037 (105662 Overseas
Highway, 305-451-0164
Key West 33040 (1350 Douglas Cir.,
305-293-4810)
Manatee 34222 (4333 U.S. Hwy 301
North, 941-721-0649)
N. Pinellas County 34619 (2465
McMullen-Booth Rd., 727-797-3789)
Oakland Park 33334 (5599 N. Dixie
Highway, 954-771-2101)
Ocala 32608 (1515 Silver Springs
Blvd., 352-369-3320)
Orlando 32803 (5201 Raymond St.,
407-629-1599, ext. 1637)
Panama City 32407 (6703 West
Hwy 98, Bldg. 387, 850-235-5101)
Pembroke Pines 33024 (2261 North
University Dr., Suite 202, 954-894-
1668)
Pensacola 32503 (312 Kenmore
Rd., 850-476-1100)
Port Richey 34668 (8911 Ponde-
rosa, 727-869-3203)
Sarasota 34233 (4000 Sawyer Rd.,
941-927-8422)
South St. Petersburg 33711 (3420
8th Avenue South, 727-322-1304)
Tallahassee 32308 (1607 St. James
Ct., 850-878-0191)

Regional Office:
St. Petersburg 33708 (9500 Bay
Pines Blvd.; statewide,1-800-827-
1000)

Benefits Offices:
Fort Myers 33901 (2070 Carrell Rd.,
1-800-827-1000)
Jacksonville 32206 (1833 Boule-
vard, Rm. 3109, 1-800-827-1000)
Miami 33130 (Federal Bldg., Rm.
120, 51 S.W. 1st Ave., 1-800-827-
1000)
Oakland Park 33334 (5599 North
Dixie Hwy., 1-800-827-1000)
Pensacola 32503-7492 (312
Kenmore Rd., Rm. 1G250, 1-800-
827-1000)

Vet Centers:
Ft. Lauderdale 33304 (713 N.E. 3rd
Ave., 954-356-7926)
Jacksonville 32202 (300 East State
St., 904-232-3621)
Miami 33129 (2700 S.W. 3rd Ave.,
Suite1A, 305-859-8387)
Orlando 32809 (5001 S. Orange
Ave., 407-857-2800)
Palm Beach 33461 (2311 10th Ave.,
North #13, 561-585-0441)
Pensacola 32501 (202 W. Jackson
St., 850-435-8761)
Sarasota 34231 (4801 Swift Rd.,
941-927-8285)
St. Petersburg 33713 (2837 1st
Ave., N., 727-893-3791)
Tallahassee 32303 (249 E. 6th Ave.,
850-942-8810)
Tampa 33604 (1507 W. Sligh Ave.,
727-228-2621)

National Cemeteries:
Barrancas 32508-1054 (Naval Air
Station, Pensacola, 850-452-
3357 or 4196)
Bay Pines 33504-0477 (P.O. Box
477, for information, call 352-793-
7740)
Florida 33513 (Bushnell, 6502 SW
102nd Avenue, 352-793-7740 or
1074)
St. Augustine 32084 (104 Marine
Street, for information, call 352-
793-7740)

GEORGIA
Medical Centers:
*Augusta 30904 (1 Freedom Way, 706-733-0188)

*Decatur 30033 (1670 Clairmont Rd., 404-321-6111)

#*Dublin 31021 (1826 Veterans Blvd., 912-272-1210)

Clinics:
Albany 31701 (521 Third Avenue, 912-446-9000)

Columbus 31906 (Medical Arts Bldg, 1310 13th Ave., 706-257-7200)

Macon 31210 (140 North Crest Blvd., 912-476-8868)

Midtown Atlanta 30309 (77 Peachtree Place, 404-321-6111, ext. 2600)

Northeast Georgia 30566 (3931 Munday Mill Road, 404-728-8210)

Savannah 31406 (325 W. Montgomery Crossroad, 912-920-0214)

Valdosta 31601 (3123 North Ashley St., 912-283-0132)

Regional Office:
Atlanta 30365 (730 Peachtree St., N.E., statewide, 1-800-827-1000)

Vet Centers:
Atlanta 30309 (77 Peachtree Pl., N.W., 404-347-7264)

Savannah 31406 (8110A White Bluff Rd., 912-652-4097)

National Cemetery:
Marietta 30060 (500 Washington Avenue, for information, call 334-855-4731)

GUAM
Clinic:
Agana Heights 96919 (U.S. Naval Hospital, 313 Farenholt Rd., 671-344-9200)

Vet Center:
Agana 96910 (222 Chalan Santo Papa St., Reflection Center, Suite 102, 671-472-7160 or 7161)

HAWAII
Medical & Regional Office:
Honolulu 96850-0001 (P.O. Box 50188, 300 Ala Moana Blvd., Rm. 1352; Medical Office, 808-566-1000; Regional Office: from Oahu, 808-566-1000; toll-free from Hawaiian neighbor islands, 1-800-827-1000; toll-free service from Guam, 475-8387; toll-free from American Samoa, 1-1-800-844-7928)

Vet Centers:
Hilo 96720 (120 Keawe St., Suite 201)

Honolulu 96814 (1680 Kapiolani Blvd., Suite F.3, 808-973-8387)

Kailua-Kona 96740 (Pottery Terrace, Fern Bldg., 75-5995 Kuakini Hwy., # 415, 808-329-0574)

Lihue 96766 (3367 Kuhlo Hwy., Suite 101, 808-246-1163)

Wailuku 96793 (35 Lunalilo, Suite 101, 808-242-8557)

National Cemetery:
National Memorial Cemetery of the Pacific (Honolulu 96813-1729, 2177 Puowaina Drive, 808-566-1430)

IDAHO
Medical Center:
*Boise 83702 (500 West Fort St., 208-422-1000)

Clinic:
Pocatello 83201 (1651 Alvin Ricken Dr., 208-232-6214)

Regional Office:
Boise 83702 (805 W. Franklin St.; statewide, 1-800-827-1000)

Vet Centers:
Boise 83705 (5440 Franklin Rd., Suite 100, 208-342-3612)

Pocatello 83201 (1800 Garrett Way, 208-232-0316)

ILLINOIS
Medical Centers:
Chicago HC System
  Lakeside Division 60611 (333 E.
  Huron St., 312-943-6600)
  Westside Division 60612 (820 S.
  Damen Ave., P.O. Box 8195, 312-
  666-6500)
*Danville 61832 (1900 E. Main St.,
  217-442-8000)
*Hines 60141 (Roosevelt Rd. & 5th
  Ave., 708-202-8387)
*Marion 62959 (2401 W. Main St.,
  618-997-5311)
#*North Chicago 60064 (3001 Green
  Bay Rd., 847-688-1900)
Clinics:
Aurora 60506 (1700 N. Landmark
  Rd., 630-859-2504)
Belleville 62223, (29 N. 64th St., 618-
  398-2100)
Decatur 62526 (3035 E. Mound Rd.,
  217-875-2670)
Effingham 62041, (301 W. Virginia,
  217-347-7600)
Elgin 60123 (1231 N. Larkin Blvd.,
  847-742-5920)
Evanston 60202 (107 -109 Clyde
  St., 847-869-6315)
Evansville, 47713 (500 E. Walnut
  St., 812-465-6202)
Galesburg 61401 (695 N. Kellogg
  St, 309-343-0311)
Gurnee 60031 (3 South Greenleaf,
  Suite J, 847-662-0978)
Joliet 60435 (2000 Glenwood Ave.,
  815-223-9678)
LaSalle 61301 (2970 Chartres St.,
  815-223-9678)
Manteno 60950 (One Veterans
  Drive, 815-468-1027)
McHenry 60050 (620 S. Route 31,
  815-759-2306)
Mt. Vernon 62864, (#1 Doctors Park
  Rd, 618-246-2911)
Oak Park 60302 (149 S. Oak Park
  Ave., 708-386-3008)

Paducah, KY CBOC 42001 (1800
  Clark St., 270-444-8465)
Peoria 61605 (411 Martin Luther
  King Jr. Dr., 309-671-7350)
Quincy 62301 (1707 North 12th St.,
  217-224-3366)
Rockford 61108 (4940 East State
  St., 815-227-0081)
Manteno 60950 (1 Veterans Dr.,
  815-468-1027)
Regional Office:
Chicago 60680 (536 S. Clark St.,
  P.O. Box 8136; statewide, 1-800-
  827-1000)
Vet Centers:
Chicago 60637 (1514 E. 63rd. St.,
  773-684-5500)
Chicago Heights 60411 (1600
  Halsted St., 708-754-0340)
East St. Louis 62203 (1269 N. 89th
  St., Suite 1, 618-397-6602)
Moline 61265 (1529 46th Ave., # 6,
  309-762-6954)
Oak Park 60302 (155 S. Oak Park
  Blvd., 708-383-3225)
Peoria 61603 (3310 N. Prospect
  Rd., 309-671-7300)
Springfield 62702 (624 S. 4th St.,
  217-492-4955)
Evanston 60202 (565 Howard St.,
  847-332-1019)
National Cemeteries:
Abraham Lincoln (Elwood, 60421,
  27034 South Diagonal Road,
  815-423-9958)
Alton 62003 (600 Pearl Street, for
  information call 314-260-8720)
Camp Butler (Springfield 62707,
  5063 Camp Butler Road,
  217-492-4070)
Danville 61832 (1900 East Main
  Street, 217-431-6550)
Mound City 62963 (P.O. Box 128, for
  information call 314-260-8720)
Quincy 62301 (36th and Maine
  Street, for information call 309-
  782-2094)

Rock Island (Moline 61265, P.O. Box
737, 309-782-2094)

INDIANA
Medical Centers:
*Indianapolis 46202 (1481 W. 10th
St., 317-554-0000)
Northern Indiana HC System:
*Fort Wayne 46805 (2121 Lake
Ave., 219-426-5431)
*Marion 46953 (1700 E. 38th St.,
765-674-3321)
Clinics:
Crown Point 46307 (9330 S.
Broadway, 219-662-0001)
Evansville 47713 (500 E. Walnut,
812-465-6202) Terre Haute 47804
(1632 North Third St., 812-232-
2890)
Lafayette 47906 (3851 N. River Rd.,
765-464-2280)
Muncie/Anderson 47304 (3500 W.
Purdue Ave., 765-284-6860)
South Bend Clinics (4 locations):
Mishawaka 46544 (201
Lincolnway West, 219-254-2799)
Mishawaka 46544 (303 South
Main #217, 219-258-0094)
Nappanee 46550 (2521 East
Market St., 219-773-4101)
South Bend 46619 (1901 Western
Ave., #B, 219-234-9033)
Regional Office:
Indianapolis 46204 (575 N. Pennsyl-
vania St.; statewide, 1-800-827-
1000)
Vet Centers:
Evansville 47711 (311 N. Weinbach
Ave., 812-473-5993 or 473-6084)
Fort Wayne 46802 (528 West Berry
St., 219-460-1456)
Highland 46322 (9105A Indianapolis
Blvd., Suite 301., 219-923-2871)
Indianapolis 46208 (3833 N.
Meridian, Suite 120, 317-927-
6440)

National Cemeteries:
Crown Hill (Indianapolis 46208, 700
W. 38th St.; for information, call
317-925-8231)
Marion 46952 (1700 E. 38th St.,
765-674-0284)
New Albany 47150 (1943 Ekin Ave.;
for information, call 502-893-3852)

IOWA
Medical Centers:
Central Iowa HC System:
#Des Moines 50310 (3600 30th &
Euclid Ave., 800-294-8387)
#*Knoxville 50138 (1515 W.
Pleasant St., 800-816-8878)
Iowa City 52246 (601 Hwy 6 West,
319-338-0581)
Clinics:
Bettendorf 52722 (2979 Victoria St.,
319-332-8528)
Dubuque 52001 (250 Mercy Dr.,
319-589-8899)
Marshalltown 50158 (1301 Summit
St, 515-753-4309)
Mason City 50401 (910 N.
Eisenhower, 515-421-4900)
Waterloo 50703 (2055 Kimball Ave,
Suite 320, 319-272-2424)
Regional Office:
Des Moines 50309 (210 Walnut St.;
statewide, 1-800-827-1000)
Vet Centers:
Cedar Rapids 52402 (1642 42nd St.
N.E., 319-378-0016)
Des Moines 50310 (2600 Martin
Luther King Jr. Pkwy.,
515-284-4929)
Sioux City 51101 (706 Jackson St.,
712-255-3808)
National Cemetery:
Keokuk 52632 (1701 J St.; for
information, call 309-782-2094)

KANSAS

Medical Centers:

Eastern Kansas HC System:
  #*Leavenworth 66048 (4101 S.
  4th St., Trafficway (913-682-2000)
  *Topeka 66622 (2200 SW Gage
  Blvd., 785-350-3111)
*Wichita 67218 (5500 E. Kellogg,
  316-685-2221)

Clinics:

Abilene 67410 (Memorial Hospital,
  510 NE 10th Street, 1-800-574-
  8387 ext. 4485)
Chanute 66720 (Neosho Memorial
  Medical Center, 629 South
  Plummer, 1-800-574-8387 ext.
  4485)
Dodge City 67801 (300 Custerm,
  316-225-7146)
Emporia 66801 (Newman Hospital,
  12th and Chestnut, 1-800-574-
  8387 ext. 4485)
Fort Riley 66442 (Irwin Army
  Hospital, Building 600, 1st Floor,
  Huebner Road 1-800-574-8387
  ext. 4485)
Garnett 66032 (Anderson County
  Hospital, 421 S. Maple, 1-800-
  574-8387 ext. 4485)
Hays 67601 (2210 Canteberry Dr.,
  785-625-5759)
Holton 66436 (Holton Community
  Hospital, 1110 Columbine Drive,
  1-800-574-8387 ext. 4485)
Junction City 66441 (Geary Commu-
  nity Hospital, Medical Arts
  Building, 1102 St. Mary's Road, 1-
  800-574-8387 ext. 4485)
Kansas City 66104 (1125 N. 5th
  Street, 800-952-8387 ext. 6990)
Lawrence 66044 (Reed Medical
  Group, 404 Maine Street, 1-800-
  574-8387 ext. 4485)
Liberal 67905 (P.O. Box 1340, 316-
  626-5574)
Paola 66071 (510 S Hospital Drive,
  816-922-2160)

Russell 67665 (Russell Regional
  Hospital, Medical Arts Building,
  200 South Main Street, 1-800-
  574-8387 ext. 4485)
St. Joseph, MO 64501 (Rosecrans
  Memorial Airport, 705 Memorial
  Drive, 816-236-3600)
Seneca 66538 (Nemaha Valley
  Community Hospital, 1600
  Community Drive, 1-800-574-
  8387, ext. 4485)

Regional Office:

Wichita 67218 (5500 E. Kellogg;
  statewide, 1-800-827-1000)

Vet Center:

Wichita 67211 (413 S. Pattie, 316-
  265-3260)

National Cemeteries:

Fort Leavenworth 66027 (For
  information, call 913-758-4105)
Fort Scott 66701 (P.O. Box 917,
  316-223-2840)
Leavenworth 66048 (P.O. Box 1694,
  913-758-4105)

KENTUCKY

Medical Centers:

*Lexington 40511 (2250 Leestown
  Rd., 606-233-4511)
Louisville 40206 (800 Zorn Ave.,
  502-895-3401)

Clinic:

Bellevue 41073 (103 Landmark Dr.,
  513-861-3100)

Regional Office:

Louisville 40202 (545 S. Third St.;
  statewide, 1-800-827-1000)

Vet Centers:

Lexington 40507 (301 E. Vine St.,
  Suite C, 606-253-0717)
Louisville 40208 (1347 S. 3rd St.,
  502-634-1916)

National Cemeteries:

Camp Nelson (Nicholasville 40356,
  6980 Danville Rd., 606-885-5727)
Cave Hill (Louisville 40204, 701
  Baxter Ave.; for information, call
  502-893-3852)

Danville 40442 (277 N. First St.; for information, call 606-885-5727)
Lebanon 40033 (20 Highway 208, call 502-692-3390)
Lexington 40508 (833 W. Main St.; for information, call 606-885-5727)
Mill Springs (Nancy 42544; for information, call 606-885-5727)
Zachary Taylor (Louisville 40207, 4701 Brownsboro Rd., 502-893-3852)

LOUISIANA
Medical Centers:
*Alexandria 71306 (P.O. Box 69004, 318-473-0010)
*New Orleans 70112 (1601 Perdido St., 504-568-0811)
Shreveport 71101 (510 E. Stoner Ave., 318-221-8411)
Clinics:
Baton Rouge 70806 (216 S. Foster Dr., 225-925-3099)
Jennings 70546 (1907 Johnson St., 337-824-1000)
Monroe 71203 (250 DeSiard Plaza, 318-343-6100)
Regional Office:
New Orleans 70113 (701 Loyola Ave., statewide, 1-800-827-1000)
Vet Centers:
New Orleans 70116 (1533 N. Claiborne Ave., 504-943-8386)
Shreveport 71104 (2800 Youree Dr., Bldg. 1, Suite 105, 318-861-1776)
National Cemeteries:
Alexandria (Pineville 71360, 209 E. Shamrock St.; for information, call 601-445-4981)
Baton Rouge 70806 (220 N. 19th St.: for information, call 225-654-3767)
Port Hudson (Zachary 70791, 20978 Port Hickey Rd., 225-654-3767)

MAINE
Medical Center:
*Togus 04330 (1 VA Center, 207-623-8411)
Regional Office:
Togus 04330 (1 VA Center, statewide, 1-800-827-1000)
Clinics:
Bangor 04401 (304 Hancock St., Suite 3B, 207-941-8160)
Calais 04619 (1 Palmer St., 207-454-7849)
Caribou 04736 (163 Van Buren Road, Suite 6, 207-498-8785)
Machias 04654 (Mobile Clinic, Upper Court St., 207-255-6063)
Rumford 04276 (209 Lincoln Ave., 207-364-4048)
Vet Centers:
Caribou 04736 (456 York St., Irving Complex, 207-496-3900)
Lewiston 04240 (Pkwy Complex, 29 Westminster St., 207-783-0068)
Portland 04103 (475 Stevens Ave., 207-780-3584)
Sanford 04073 (352 Harlow St., 207-490-1513, fax 207-490-1609)
Springvale 04083 (23 Main St., 207-490-1513)
National Cemetery:
Togus 04330 (VA Medical and Regional Office Center; for information, call 508-563-7113)

MARYLAND
Medical Centers:
Maryland HC System:
 *Baltimore 21201 (10 N. Green St., 410-605-7000)
 Fort Howard 21052 (9600 N. Point Rd., 410-477-1800)
 #Perry Point 21902 (410-642-2411)
Baltimore 21201 (Prosthetic Assessment Information Center, 103 S. Gay St., 410-962-3934)

Clinics:

Cumberland 21502 (710 Memorial Ave., 301-724-0061)

Hagerstown 21742 (1500 Pennsylvania Avenue, 301-665-1462)

Regional Office:

Baltimore 21201 (31 Hopkins Plaza Fed. Bldg., l-800-827-1000; counties of Montgomery, Prince Georges served by Washington, DC, RO, 1-800-827-1000)

Vet Centers:

Baltimore 21207 (6666 Security Blvd., Suite 2, 410-277-3600)

Elkton 21921 (7 Elkton Commercial Plaza, South Bridge St., 410-398-0171)

Silver Spring 20910 (1015 Spring St., Suite 101, 301-589-1073)

National Cemeteries:

Annapolis 21401 (800 West St.; for information, call 410-644-9696)

Baltimore 21228 (5501 Frederick Ave., 410-644-9696)

Loudon Park (Baltimore 21228, 3445 Frederick Ave.; for information, call 410-644-9696)

MASSACHUSETTS

Medical Centers:

Bedford 01730 (200 Springs Rd., 1-800-VETMED1, or 781-687-2275)

Boston 02130 (150 S. Huntington Ave., 617-232-9500)

Brockton 02301, 940 Belmont St., 508-583-4500)

West Roxbury 02132 (1400 VFW Pkwy., 617-323-7700)

*Northampton 01053-9764 (421 N. Main St., 413-584-4040)

Clinics:

Boston 02114 (251 Causeway St., 617-248-1000)

Framingham 01702 (61 Lincoln St., 508 628-0205)

Haverhill 01830 (140 Lincoln Ave., 978-372-5207)

Hyannis 02601 (145 Falmouth Rd., 508 771-3190)

Lynn 01904 (225 Boston Street, Suite 107, 781-595-9818)

Lowell 01852 (81 Bridge St., 978-934-9124)

Lowell 01852 (130 Marshall Rd., 978-671-9000)

New Bedford 02740 (175 Elm St., 508 994-0217)

Pittsfield 01201 (73 Eagle St., 413-443-4857)

Springfield 01103 (1550 Main St., 413-785-0301)

Winchendon 01475 (Streeter School, Murdock Ave., 978-297-3028)

Worcester 01605 (605 Lincoln St., 508-856-0104)

Regional Office:

Boston 02203 (JFK Federal Bldg., Government Center; statewide, 1-800-827-1000) Towns of Fall River & New Bedford, counties of Barnstable, Dukes, Nantucket, Bristol, part of Plymouth served by Providence, R.I., RO)

Vet Centers:

Boston 02215 (665 Beacon St., 617-424-0665)

Brockton 02401 (1041-L Pearl St., 508-580-2730)

Lowell 01852 (73 East Merrimack St., 978-453-1151)

New Bedford 02740 (468 North St., 508-999-6920)

Springfield 01103 (1985 Main St., Northgate Plaza, 413-737-5167)

Worcester 01605 (597 Lincoln St., 508-856-7428)

National Cemetery:

Massachusetts (Bourne 02532, off Connery Ave. 508-563-7113)

MICHIGAN

Medical Centers:

*Ann Arbor 48105 (2215 Fuller Rd., 734-769-7100)

*Battle Creek 49016 (5500
  Armstrong Rd., 616-966-5600)
*Detroit 48201 (4646 John R. St.,
  313-576-1000)
*Iron Mountain 49801 (325 E. H St.,
  906-774-3300 or 1-800-215-8262
  in Mich. and Wis.)
*Saginaw 48602 (1500 Weiss St.,
  517-793-2340)

Clinics:
Gaylord 49735 (806 S. Otsego,
  517-732-6555)
Grand Rapids 49505 (3019 Coit,
  N.E., 616-365-9575)
Hancock 49930-1495 (890 Campus
  Dr.,906-482-7762)
Ironwood 49938 (Grandview
  Rd.,906-932-1500)
Jackson 49202 (2200 Springport
  Rd., 517-787-8010)
Lansing 48910 (2727 S. Pennsylva-
  nia, 517-374-4295)
Marquette 49855 (425 Fisher Street,
  906-226-4618)
Menominee 49858 (1101 11th Ave.,
  Suite 2, 906-863-1286)
Muskegon 49442 (165 E. Apple
  Ave., 616-725-4105)
Sault Ste. Marie 49783 (2864
  Ashmun Rd., 906-253-9564)
Traverse City 49648 (745 S.
  Garfield, 231-932-9720)
Yale 48097 (7470 Brockway Rd.,
  810-387-3211)

Regional Office:
Detroit 48226 (Patrick V. McNamara
  Federal Bldg., 477 Michigan Ave.;
  statewide,1-800-827-1000)

Vet Centers:
Grand Rapids 49507 (165 E. Apple
  Ave., Suite 201, Bldg. F, 616-243-
  0385)
Lincoln Park 48146 (1766 Fort St.,
  313-381-1370)
Detroit 48201 (4161 Cass Ave.,
  313-831-6509)

National Cemetery:
Fort Custer (Augusta 49012, 15501
  Dickman Rd., 616-731-4164)

MINNESOTA
Medical Centers:
*Minneapolis 55417 (One Veterans
  Dr., 612-725-2000)
#*St. Cloud 56303 (4801 8th St.
  North, 320-252-1670 or 1-800-
  247-1739)

Clinics:
Fergus Falls 56537 (1821 North
  Park Street, 218-739-1400)
Maplewood 55109 (2785 White Bear
  Ave., Suite 210, 651-290-3040)
Brainerd 56401 (1777 Hwy 18 East,
  218-855-1115)
Mankato Area (612-725-2000)
Hibbing Area (612-725-2000)

Reg.Office and Ins.Center:
St. Paul 55111 (Bishop Henry
  Whipple Federal Bldg., 1 Federal
  Dr., Fort Snelling; statewide, 1-
  800-827-1000)
Counties of Becker, Beltrami, Clay,
  Clearwater, Kittson, Lake of the
  Woods, Mahnomen, Marshall,
  Norman, Otter Tail, Pennington,
  Polk, Red Lake, Roseau, Wilkin
  served by Fargo, N.D., RO)

Vet Centers:
Duluth 55802 (405 E. Superior St.,
  218-722-8654)
St. Paul 55114 (2480 University
  Ave., 651-644-4022)

National Cemetery:
Fort Snelling (Minneapolis 55450-
  1199, 7601 34th Ave. So.,
  612-726-1127)

MISSISSIPPI
Medical Centers:
#*Biloxi 39531 (400 Veterans Ave.,
  228-523-5000)
*Jackson 39216 (1500 E. Woodrow
  Wilson Dr., 601-362-4471)

Regional Office:
Jackson 39269 (1600 E. Woodrow
Willson Ave., 1-800-827-1000)
Vet Centers:
Biloxi 39531 (313 Abbey Ct., 228-
388-9938)
Jackson 39206 (4436 N. State St.,
Suite A3, 601-965-5727)
National Cemeteries:
Biloxi 39535-4968 (P.O. Box 4968,
228-388-6668)
Corinth 38834 (1551 Horton St.; for
information, call 901-386-8311)
Natchez 39120 (41 Cemetery Rd.,
601-445-4981)

MISSOURI
Medical Centers:
*Columbia 65201 (800 Hospital Dr.,
573-443-2511)
Kansas City 64128 (4801 Linwood
Blvd., 816-861-4700)
*Poplar Bluff 63901 (1500 N.
Westwood Blvd., 573-686-4151)
St. Louis 63106 (John Cochran Div.,
915 N. Grand Blvd., 314-652-
4100)
*St. Louis 63125 (#1 Jefferson
Barracks Div., 314-487-0400)
Clinics:
Belton 64021 (17140 Bel-Ray Place,
816-922-2161)
Cape Girardeau 63701 (1923 N.
Kingshighway, 573-339-0909)
Mt. Vernon 65712 (600 N. Main St.,
417-466-4000)
Nevada 64772, (322 Prewitt, 816-
922-2163)
St. Charles 63304, (#7 Jason Court,
636-498-1113)
West Plains 65775, (1438 BB
Highway, 417-257-2454)
Whiteman AFB 65305, (331 Sijan
Ave, 816-922-2162)
Regional Office:
St. Louis 63103 (400 South 18th St.;
statewide, 1-800-827-1000)

Benefits Office:
Kansas City 64106 (Federal Office
Bldg., 601 E. 12th St., 1-800-827-
1000)
Vet Centers:
Kansas City 64111 (3931 Main St.,
816-753-1866)
St. Louis 63103 (2345 Pine St., 314-
231-1260)
National Cemeteries:
Jefferson Barracks (St. Louis 63125,
2900 Sheridan Rd.,
314-260-8720)
Jefferson City 65101 (1024 E.
McCarty St.; for information, call
314-260-8720)
Springfield 65804 (1702 E. Seminole
St., 417-881-9499)

MONTANA
**Medical Centers & Regional
Office:**
Montana HC System
Fort Harrison 59636 (William St.
off Hwy. 12 W.; Medical Center,
406-442-6410; Regional Office, 1-
800-827-1000)
*Miles City 59301 (210 S. Win-
chester, 406-232-3060)
Clinic:
Billings 59102 (2345 King Ave. W.,
406-651-5670)
Vet Centers:
Billings 59102 (1234 Avenue C, 406-
657-6071)
Missoula 59801 (500 N. Higgins
Ave., 406-721-4918)

NEBRASKA
Medical Centers:
VA Nebraska:
*Grand Island 68803 (2201 N.
Broadwell Ave., 308-382-3660)
Lincoln 68510 (600 S. 70th St.,
402-489-3802)
Omaha 68105 (4101 Woolworth
Ave, 402-346-8800)

Clinics:
Norfolk 68701 (2600 Norfolk Ave., Suite B, 402-346-8800)
North Platte 69101 (220 W. Leota St., 308-532-6906)
Regional Office:
Lincoln 68516 (5631 S. 48th St., statewide, 1-800-827-1000)
Vet Centers:
Lincoln 68508 (920 L St., 402-476-9736)
Omaha 68131 (2428 Cuming St., 402-346-6735)
National Cemetery:
Fort McPherson (Maxwell 69151, HCO 1, Box 67, 308-582-4433)

NEVADA
Medical Centers:
Las Vegas 89106 (1700 Vegas Dr., 702-636-3000)
*Reno 89520 (1000 Locust St., 1-888-838-6256)
Clinics:
Henderson 89014 (2920 N. Green Valley Parkway, Suite 215, 702-456-3825)
Pahrump 89048 (1501 E. Calvada Blvd., 702-727-6060)
Regional Office:
Reno 89520 (1201 Terminal Way, statewide, 1-800-827-1000)
Benefits Office:
Las Vegas 89107(4800 Alpine Pl., Suite 11, 1-800-827-1000)
Vet Centers:
Las Vegas 89104 (1040 E. Sahara Ave., Suite 102, 702-388-6369)
Reno 89503 (1155 W. 4th St., Suite 101, 775-323-1294)

NEW HAMPSHIRE
Medical Center:
*Manchester 03104 (718 Smyth Rd., 603-624-4366 or 1-800-892-8384)

Clinics:
Portsmouth 03803 (302 Newmarket St., Building 15, 603-624-4366 or 1-800-892-8384)
Tilton 03276 (139 Winter St., 603-624-4366 or 1-800-892-8384)
Regional Office:
Manchester 03101 (Norris Cotton Federal Bldg., 275 Chestnut St.; statewide, 1-800-827-1000)
Vet Center:
Manchester 03104 (103 Liberty St., 603-668-7060/61)

NEW JERSEY
Medical Centers:
New Jersey HC System:
    *East Orange 07018 (385 Tremont Ave., 973-676-1000)
    #*Lyons 07939 (151Knollkroft Rd., 908-647-0180)
Clinics:
Brick 08724 (970 Rt. 70, 732-206-8900)
Cape May 08204 (1 Monroe Avenue, 609-898-8700)
Elizabeth 07201 (654 East Jersey St., 908-994-0120)
Ft. Dix 08640 (Marshall Hall, 8th & Alabama, 609-562-2999)
Hackensack 07601 (385 Prospect Ave., 201-487-1390)
Jersey City 07302 (115 Christopher Columbus Dr., 201-435-3055)
New Brunswick 08901 (317 George St., 732-729-9555)
Trenton 08611 (171 Jersey St, Bldg. 36, 609-989-2355)
Ventnor 08406 (6601 Ventnor Ave., Suite 406, 609-823-3122)
Vineland 08240 (NJ Veterans Memorial Home, Northwest Blvd., 609-823-3122)
Regional Office:
Newark 07102 (20 Washington Pl., statewide, 1-800-827-1000)

Vet Centers:

Jersey City 07302 (115 Christopher Columbus Dr., Rm., 200, 973-645-2038)

Newark 07102 (157 Washington St., 973-645-5954)

Trenton 08611 (171 Jersey St., Bldg. 36, 609-989-2260)

Ventnor 08406 (6601 Ventnor Ave., Suite 401, 609-487-8387)

National Cemeteries:

Beverly 08010 (R.D. # 1, Bridgeboro Rd., 609-877-5460)

Finn's Point (Salem 08079, R.F.D. 3, Fort Mott Rd., Box 542; for information, call 609-877-5460)

NEW MEXICO

Medical Center:

*Albuquerque 87108 (1501 San Pedro Dr., SE., 505-265-1711)

Clinics:

Artesia 88210 (1700 W. Main St., 505-746-3531)

Clovis 88101 (100 E. Manana St., Suite 1, 505-763-4335)

Clayton 88415 (301 Harding, 505-374-2585)

Farmington 87401 (1001C W. Broadway, 505-326-4383)

Gallup 87301 (1806 E. 66th Ave., #5, 505-722-7234)

Hobbs 88240 (1601 N. Turner, 505-391-0354)

Las Cruces CBOC 88001 (1635 Don Roser, 505-522-1241)

Raton 87740 (1275 S. 2nd St., 505-445-2391)

Silver City 88061 (1302 32nd St., 505-538-2921)

Regional Office:

Albuquerque 87102 (Dennis Chavez Federal Bldg., 500 Gold Ave., S.W.; statewide, 1-800-827-1000)

Vet Centers:

Albuquerque 87104 (1600 Mountain Rd. N.W., 505-346-6562)

Farmington 87402 (4251 E. Main, Suite B, 505-327-9684)

Santa Fe 87505 (2209 Brothers Rd., Suite 110, 505-988-6562)

National Cemeteries:

Fort Bayard 88036 (P.O. Box 189; for information, call Fort Bliss, TX, 915-564-0201)

Santa Fe 87501 (501 N. Guadalupe St., 505-988-6400)

NEW YORK

Medical Centers:

*Albany 12208 (113 Holland Ave., 518-462-3311)

#*Bath 14810 (76 Veterans Ave., 607-776-2111)

*Bronx 10468 (130 W. Kingsbridge Rd., 718-584-9000)

NY Harbor Healthcare System:

#*Brooklyn 11209 (800 Poly Place, 718-836-6600)

New York 10010 (423 East 23rd St. (1st Ave.), 212-686-7500)

St. Albans 11425 (179 Street & Linden Blvd., 718-526-1000)

#*Canandaigua 14424 (400 Fort Hill Ave., 716-394-2000)

Hudson Valley HC System:

#*Montrose 10548 (138 Albany Post Rd., 914-737-4400)

*Castle Point 12511 (Rte. 9D, 914-831-2000)

*Northport 11768 (79 Middleville Rd., 631-261-4400)

*Syracuse 13210 (800 Irvine Ave., 315-476-7461)

Western New York HC System:

*Buffalo 14215 (3495 Bailey Ave., 716-834-9200)

*Batavia 14020 (222 Richmond Ave., 716-343-7500)

Clinics:

Alexandria Bay 13607 (21 Fuller Street, 315-482-4466)

Bennington 05201 (325 North Street, 802-477-6913)

Binghamton 13001 (425 Robinson Street, 607-772-9100)

Brooklyn 11201 (Chapel Street Center, 40th Flatbush Avenue Ext., 8th Floor, 718-439-4300)

Buffalo 14209 (St. Vincent De Paul, 1298 Main Street, 716-551-3800)

Buffalo 14214 (2963 Main St., 716-834-4270)

Clifton Park 12065 (1673 Route 9, 518-383-8506)

Dunkirk 14048 (The Resources Center, 325 Central Ave., 716-366-2122)

Elizabethtown 12932 (Community Hospital, Park St., 518-873-2179)

Glens Falls 12801 (84 Broad Street, 518-798-6066)

Islip 11751 (39 Nassau Ave., 631-581-5330)

Jamestown 14701 (The Resources Center, 896 East 2nd Street, 716-661-1447)

Kingston 12401 (63 Hurley Avenue, 914-331-8322)

Lindenhurst 11757 (560 N. Delaware Ave., 516-884-1133)

Lockport 14304 (Ambulatory Care Center, 5875 S. Transit Road, 716-433-2025)

Lynbrook 11563 (235 Merrick Rd., 516-887-3666)

Malone 12953 (115 Park Street, 518-481-2545)

Massena 13662 (1 Hospital Dr., 315-764-1711)

Mt. Sinai 11766 (Mt. Sinai Community Ctr., N. Country Rd., 631-473-4068)

New York 10027 (Harlem Center, 55 West 125th Street, 11th Floor, 212-828-5265)

New York 10014 (Soho Center, 245 West Houston Street, 212-337-2569)

Niagara Falls 14304 (Horizon Health Service, 6560 Niagara Falls Blvd, 716-283-2000)

Oswego 13126 (Seneca Hill Health Services Center, County Route 45A, 315-343-0925)

Patchogue 11772 (269 Baker St. and S. Ocean Ave., 631-475-6610)

Plainview 11803 (1535 Old Country Rd., 516-572-8567)

Plattsburgh 12901 (206 Cornelia Street, Medical Bldg. Suite 307, 518-566-8563)

Riverhead 11901 (89 Hubbard Ave., 631-727-7171)

Rochester 14620 (465 Westfall Rd., 716-242-0160)

Rome 13441 (125 Brookley Road, Building 510, 315-366-3389)

Sayville 11782 (400 Lakeland Ave., 631-563-1105)

Schenectady 12309 (1475 Balltown Road, 518-346-3334)

Sidney 13838 (39 Pearl St. West, 607-561-2003)

Staten Island 10304 (Staten Island Center, 21 Water Street, 718-815-2500)

Troy 12180 (500 Federal Street, 518-274-7707)

Warsaw 14569 (Warsaw Satellite Site, 338 N. Main Street, 716-344-3355)

Watertown 13601 (1575 Washington Street, 315-779-5050)

White Plains 20601 (23 South Broadway,914-421-1951)

Yonkers, NY 10705 (118 New Main Street, 914-375-8055)

Regional Offices:

Buffalo 14202 (Federal Bldg., 111 W. Huron St.; statewide, 1-800-827-1000)
Serves counties not served by New York City Regional Office.

New York City 10014 (245 W. Houston St.; statewide, 1-800-827-1000) Serves counties of Albany, Bronx, Clinton, Columbia, Delaware, Dutchess, Essex,

Franklin, Fulton, Greene,
Hamilton, Kings, Montgomery,
Nassau, New York, Orange,
Otsego, Putnam, Queens,
Rensselaer, Richmond, Rockland,
Saratoga, Schenectady,
Schoharie, Suffolk, Sullivan,
Ulster, Warren, Washington,
Westchester.

Benefits Offices:
Rochester 14620 (465 Westfall Rd.,,
1-800-827-1000)
Syracuse 13202 (344 W. Genesee
St., 1-800-827-1000)

Vet Centers:
Albany 12206 (875 Central Ave.,
518-438-2505)
Babylon 11702 (116 West Main St.,
631-661-3930)
Brooklyn 11201 (25 Chapel St.,
Suite 604, 718-330-2825)
Bronx 10458 (226 E. Fordham Rd.,
Room 220, 718-367-3500)
Buffalo 14202 (560 Delaware Ave.,
Suite 1, 716-882-0505)
Harlem 10036 (120 W. 44th St., 212-
426-2200)
New York 10027 (55 West 125th St.,
212- 828-5265, 212-426-2200)
Rochester 14604 (205 St. Paul St.,
716-232-5040)
Staten Island 10301 (150 Richmond
Terrace, 718-816-4799)
Syracuse 13210 (716 E. Washington
St., 315-478-7127)
White Plains 10601 (300 Hamilton
Ave., 914-682-6251)
Woodhaven 11421 (75-10B 91st
Ave., 718-296-2871)

National Cemeteries:
Bath 14810 (VA Medical Center,
607-776-5480, ext. 1293)
Calverton 11933-1031 (210
Princeton Blvd., 631-727-5410)
Cypress Hills (Brooklyn 11208, 625
Jamaica Ave.; for information, call
631-454-4949)

Long Island (Farmingdale 11735-
1211, 2040 Wellwood Ave.,
631-454-4949)
Saratoga (Schuylerville 12871-1721,
200 Duell Road, 518-581-9128)
Woodlawn (Elmira 14901, 1825
Davis St.; for information, call
607-776-5480, ext. 1293)

NORTH CAROLINA
Medical Centers:
*Asheville 28805 (1100 Tunnel Rd.,
828-298-7911)
*Durham 27705 (508 Fulton St.,
919-286-0411)
*Fayetteville 28301 (2300 Ramsey
St., 910-488-2120)
*Salisbury 28144 (1601 Brenner
Ave., 704-638-9000)

Clinics:
Charlotte 28213 (101 W.T. Harris
Blvd. Bldg. 1000 Suite 1214, 704-
594-9152)
Greenville 27858 (800 Moye Blvd.,
252-830-2149)
Jacksonville 28546 (121 Memorial
Drive, 910-577-2883)
Winston-Salem 27103 (190 Kimel
Park Dr., 336-768-3296, ext. 1209
or 1210)

Regional Office:
Winston-Salem 27155 (Federal
Bldg., 251 N. Main St., statewide,
1-800-827-1000)

Vet Centers:
Charlotte 28202 (223 S. Brevard St.,
Suite 103, 704-333-6107)
Fayetteville 28311 (4140 Ramsey
St., Suite 110, 910-488-6252)
Greensboro 27406 (2009 S. Elm-
Eugene St., 336-333-5366)
Greenville 27858 (150 Arlington
Blvd., Suite B, 252-355-7920)
Raleigh 27604 (1649 Old Louisburg
Rd., 919-856-4616)

National Cemeteries:
New Bern 28560 (1711 National
Ave., 252-637-2912)

Raleigh 27610 (501 Rock Quarry Rd.; for information, call 704-636-2661)

Salisbury 28144 (202 Government Rd., 704-636-2661)

Wilmington 28403 (2011 Market St.; for information, call 252-637-2912)

NORTH DAKOTA
Medical and Regional Office:
*Fargo 58102 (2101 N. Elm St.; Medical Center 701-232-3241; Regional Office; statewide, 1-800-827-1000)

Clinics:
Minot 58705 (10 Missile Avenue, 701-727-9800)

Bismarck 58506 (701-232-3241)

Grafton 58237 (West 6th Street, 701-352-4594)

Vet Centers:
Fargo 58103 (3310 Fiechtner Dr., Suite 100, 701-237-0942)

Minot 58701 (2041 3rd St. N.W., 701-852-0177)

Bismarck 58501 (1684 Capital Way, 701-244-9751)

OHIO
Medical Centers:
#*Brecksville 44141 (10000 Brecksville Rd., 440-526-3030)

*Chillicothe 45601 (17273 State Route 104, 740-773-1141)

#*Cincinnati 45220 (3200 Vine St., 513-861-3100)

Cleveland 44106, (10701 East Blvd., 216-791-3800)

#*Dayton 45428 (4100 W. 3rd St., 937-268-6511)

Clinics:
Akron 44311 (676 S. Broadway St., 330-344-4177)

Ashtabula 44004 (4314 Main Ave., 814-868-8661)

Athens 45701 (510 W. Union St., 740-593-7314)

Canton 44702 (221 Third St., S.E., 330-489-4660)

Cleveland/McCafferty 44113 (4242 Lorain Ave., 216-939-0699)

Cleveland/Otis Moss 44106 (8819 Quincy Ave., 216-721-7221)

Columbus 43203 (543 Taylor Ave., 614-257-5200)

Lorain 44052 (205 W. 20th St., 440-244-3833)

Mansfield 44906 (1456 Park Avenue West, 419-529-4602)

Middletown 45042 (675 N. University Blvd., 513-423-8387)

Painesville 44077 (54 S. State St., 440-357-6740)

Portsmouth 45662 (621 Broadway St., 740-353-3236)

St. Clairsville 43950 (51339 National Road East, 614-695-9321)

Sandusky 44870 (3416 Columbus Ave., 419-625-7350)

Springfield 45505 (512 S. Burnett Rd., 937-328-3385)

Toledo 43614 (3333 Glendale Ave., 419-259-2000)

Youngstown 44505 (2031 Belmont, 330-740-9200)

Zanesville 43701 (840 Bethesda Dr., 740-453-7725)

Regional Office:
Cleveland 44199 (Anthony J. Celebrezze Federal Bldg., 1240 E. 9th St.; statewide, 1-800-827-1000)

Benefits Offices:
Cincinnati 45202 (36 E. Seventh St., Suite 210, 1-800-827-1000)

Columbus 43215 (Federal Bldg., Rm. 309, 200 N. High St., 1-800-827-1000)

Vet Centers:
Cincinnati 45203 (801-B W. 8th St., 513-763-3500)

Cleveland Heights 44118 (2022 Lee Rd., 216-932-8471)

Columbus 43215 (30 Spruce St., 614-257-5550)

Dayton 45402 (111 W 3rd St., Suite 101, 937-461-9150)

Parma 44129 (5700 Pearl Rd., Suite 102, 440-845-5023

National Cemeteries:
Dayton 45428-1008 (VA Medical Center, 4100 W. Third St., 937-262-2115)

Ohio Western Reserve (Rittman 44270, P.O. Box 8, 10175 Rawiga Road, 330-335-3069, open Spring 2000)

OKLAHOMA
Medical Centers:
Muskogee 74401 (1011 Honor Heights Dr., 918-683-3261)

*Oklahoma City 73104 (921 N.E. 13th St., 405-270-0501)

Clinics:
Ardmore 73401 (1015 S. Commerce, 580-223-2266)

Bonham Area (Red River, Bryan, Choctaw and McCurtain Counties, 800-924-8387, ext. 6342 or commercial 903-583-6342)

Clinton 73601 (1/4 mile south of I-40 on Highway 183, P.O. Box 1209)

Lawton/Ft. Sill 43503 (Bldg. 4303, 4303 Pittman and Thomas, 580-353-1131)

Tulsa 74127 (635 W. 11th St., 918-764-7243)

Regional Office:
Muskogee 74401 (Federal Bldg., 125 S. Main St.; statewide, 1-800-827-1000)

Benefits Office:
Oklahoma City 73102 (215 Dean A. McGee Ave., Room 276, 1-800-827-1000)

Vet Centers:
Oklahoma City 73105 (3033 N. Walnut, Suite 101W, 405-270-5184)

Tulsa 74112 (1408 S. Harvard, 918-748-5105)

National Cemetery:
Fort Gibson 74434 (1423 Cemetery Rd., 918-478-2334)

OREGON
Medical Centers:
#*Portland 97201 (3710 S.W. U.S. Veterans Hospital Rd., 503-220-8262)

*Roseburg 97470 (913 N.W. Garden Valley Blvd.,541-440-1000)

Clinics:
Bend 97701 (2042 Williamson Court, Suite 100, 503-220-8262)

Bandon 97411 (1010 1st St. S.E., Suite 100, 541-347-4736)

Eugene 97404 (100 River Ave., 541-607-0897)

Domiciliary:
White City 97503 (8495 Crater Lake Hwy., 541-826-2111, ext. 3210 or 3239, 1-800-809-8725)

Regional Office:
Portland 97204 (Federal Bldg., 1220 S.W. 3rd Ave.; statewide, 1-800-827-1000)

Vet Centers:
Eugene 97403 (1255 Pearl St., 541-465-6918)

Grants Pass 97526 (211 S.E. 10th St., 541-479-6912)

Portland 97220 (8383 N.E. Sandy Blvd., Suite 110, 503-273-5370)

Salem 97301 (617 Chemeketa St., N.E., 503-362-9911)

National Cemeteries:
Eagle Point 97524 (2763 Riley Rd., 541-826-2511)

Roseburg 97470 (VA Medical Center; for information, call 541-826-2511)

Willamette (Portland 97266-6937, 11800 S.E. Mt. Scott Blvd., 503-273-5250)

PENNSYLVANIA
Medical Centers:
*Altoona 16602 (2907 Pleasant
Valley Blvd., 814-943-8164)

#*Butler 16001 (325 New Castle
Rd., 724-287-4781)

#*Coatesville 19320 (1400 Black
Horse Hill Rd., 610-384-7711)

*Erie 16504-1596 (135 E. 38th St.,
814-868-8661)

*Lebanon 17042 (1700 S. Lincoln
Ave., 717-272-6621)

*Philadelphia 19104 (University &
Woodland Aves., 215-823-5800)

Pittsburgh HC System:
*Pittsburgh 15240 (University
Drive C, 412-688-6000, toll-free 1-
800-309-8398)

Pittsburgh 15240 (Delafield Road,
412-688-6000, toll-free 1-800-309-
8398)

#Pittsburgh 15206 (7180
Highland Dr., 412-363-4900, toll-free
1-800-647-6220)

*Wilkes-Barre 18711 (1111 East End
Blvd.,1-877-928-2621, toll-free)

Clinics:
Aliquippa 15001 (2415 Broadhead
Rd.) 724-378-6640)

Allentown 18103 (3110 Hamilton
Blvd., 610-776-4304)

Camp Hill 17011 (25 N. 23rd St.,
717-783-9782)

DuBois 15801 (90 Beaver Dr., Rice
Complex, Building D, Suite 213,
814-375-6817)

Frackville 17931 (Good Samaritan
Health Center, 602 Altamount
Blvd, 570-462-2783)

Greensburg 15601 (RR#6 Box 112,
724-830-8762)

Johnstown 15904 (108 College Park
Plaza, 814-266-8696)

Lancaster 17605 (Greenfield
Corporate Center, 1861 Charter
Lane, 717-290-6905)

Levittown 19055 (7321 New Falls
Rd, 215-547-3423)

Meadville 16335 (279 Walnut Street,
814-868-8661)

Reading 19601 (145 N. Sixth Street,
610-208-4717)

Sayre 18840 (301 N. Elmira, 570-
888-8062)

State College 16801 (3048 Enter-
prise Dr., Ferguson Square, 814-
867-5415)

Schuylkill County 17901 (700 E.
Norwegian St., 570-621-4561)

Schuylkill Haven 17972 (Rt. 61
South, 570-366-3915)

Smethport 16749 (406 Franklin St,
814-887-5655)

Spring City 19475 (11 Independence
Drive, 610-948-0981)

Springfield 19064 (489 Baltimore
Pike, 610-543-1588)

Tobyhanna 18466 (Bldg. 220,
Tobyhanna Army Depot, 717-895-
8341)

Williamsport 17701 (805 Penn St.,
717-322-4791)

Regional Offices:
Philadelphia 19144 (RO and
Insurance Center, P.O. Box 8079,
5000 Wissahickon Ave., RO, 1-
800-827-1000; insurance, local,
842-2000, nationwide1-800-669-
8477; Serves counties of Adams,
Berks, Bradford, Bucks, Cameron,
Carbon, Centre, Chester, Clinton,
Columbia, Cumberland, Dauphin,
Delaware, Franklin, Juniata,
Lackawanna, Lancaster, Lebanon,
Lehigh, Luzerne, Lycoming,
Mifflin, Monroe, Montgomery,
Montour, Northampton,
Northumberland, Perry, Philadel-
phia, Pike, Potter, Schuylkill,
Snyder, Sullivan, Susquehanna,
Tioga, Union, Wayne, Wyoming,
York.

Pittsburgh 15222 (1000 Liberty Ave.;
statewide, 1-800-827-1000,
Serves the remaining counties of
Pennsylvania.)

Benefits Office:
Wilkes-Barre 18702 (Jewelcor Bldg., 2nd Floor, 100 N. Wilkes-Barre Blvd., 1-800-827-1000)
Vet Centers:
Erie 16501 (1001 State St., Suite 1&2, 814-453-7955)
Harrisburg 17102 (1007 N. Front St., 717-782-3954)
McKeesport 15132 (2001 Lincoln Way., 412-678-7704)
Philadelphia 19107 (801 Arch St., Suite 102, 215-627-0238)
Philadelphia 19152 (101 E. Olney Ave., Box C-7, 215-924-4670)
Pittsburgh 15222 (954 Penn Ave., 412-765-1193)
Scranton 18505 (1002 Pittston Ave., 570-344-2676)
Williamsport 17701 (805 Penn St., 570-327-5281)
National Cemeteries:
Indiantown Gap (Annville 17003-9618, R.R. 2, P.O. Box 484, 717-865-5254)
Philadelphia 19138 (Haines St. & Limekiln Pike; for information, call 609-877-5460)

PHILIPPINES
Regional Office:
Manila 0930 (1131 Roxas Blvd., 011-632-523-1001)(International Mailing Address: PSC 501,FPO AP 96515-1100)
Outpatient Clinic:
Manila 1300 (2201 Roxas Blvd., Pasay City, 011-632-833-4566)

PUERTO RICO
Medical Center:
*San Juan 00927 (10 Casia St., 787-766-5599)
Clinics:
Arecibo (Galle Gonzalo Marin #50, 787-816-1824)

Mayaguez 00680 (Ave. Hostos 345, Frente Vista Verde Plaza; 787-834-6900, 1-800-569-2356)
Ponce 00731 (Reparada Industrial-Lot #1, Calle Principal, 787-841-3106)
St. Croix 00850 (Box 12, RR-02 The Village Mall #13, Kingshill, U.S.VI, 340-778-5553)
St. Thomas 00802 (Bucaneer Mall #8 St. Thomas U.S. VI, 340-774-6674)
Regional Office:
San Juan 00918 (150 Carlos Chardon Ave., Hato Rey; For mail: P. O. Box 364867, San Juan, PR 00936. All Puerto Rico and the Virgin Islands, 1-800-827-1000)
Benefits Offices:
Ponce 00731 (Ponce Outpatient Clinic, Urb. Industrial Reparada, Lote 1 Calle Principal, 1-800-827-1000)
Mayaguez 00680 (Mayaguez Outpatient Clinic, Ave. Hostos 345 Carretera 2, Frente al Centro Medico, 1-800-827-1000)
Vet Centers:
Arecibo 00612-4702 (52 Gonzalo Marin St., 787-879-4510 or 879-4581)
Ponce 00731 (35 Mayor St., 787-841-3260)
San Juan 00921 (Condominio Medical Center Plaza, Suite LC8A and LC9, La Riviera, 787-749-4409)
National Cemetery:
Bayamon 00960 (Avenue Cementerio Nacional #50, Barrio Hato Tejas, 787-798-7620)

RHODE ISLAND
Medical Center:
Providence 02908 (830 Chalkstone Ave., 401-273-7100)

Regional Office:
Providence 02903 (380 Westminster St.; statewide, 1-800-827-1000)
Vet Center:
Cranston 02910 (789 Park Ave., 401-467-2046)

SOUTH CAROLINA
Medical Centers:
Charleston 29401 (109 Bee St., 843-577-5011)
*Columbia 29209 (6439 Garners Ferry Rd., 803-776-4000)
Clinics:
Florence OPC 29501 (514H Dargan St., 843-292-8383)
Greenville 29605 (3510 Augusta Rd., 864-299-1600)
Myrtle Beach Primary Care Clinic 29577 (3381 Phillis Blvd., 843-477-0177)
Rock Hill OPC 29732 (124 Glenwood St., 803-328-3622)
Regional Office:
Columbia 29201 (1801 Assembly St.; statewide, 1-800-827-1000)
Vet Centers:
Columbia 29201 (1513 Pickens St., 803-765-9944)
Greenville 29601 (14 Lavinia Ave., 864-271-2711)
North Charleston 29406 (5603A Rivers Ave., 843-747-8387)
Savannah 31406 (8110A White Bluff Rd., 912-652-4097)
National Cemeteries:
Beaufort 29902 (1601 Boundary St., 843-524-3925)
Florence 29501 (803 E. National Cemetery Rd., 843-669-8783)

SOUTH DAKOTA
Medical Centers:
Black Hills HC System:
*Fort Meade 57741 (113 Comanche Rd., 605-347-2511 or 1-800-743-1070)
#Hot Springs 57747 (500 North 5th Street, 605-745-2000 or 1-800-764-5370)
*Sioux Falls 57117 (2501 W. 22nd St., 605-336-3230)
Clinics:
Rapid City 57701 (2823 West Main St., 605-399-6655 or 1-800-743-1070)
Pierre 57501 (1601 N. Harrison, 1-800-743-1070)
Regional Office:
Sioux Falls 57117 (P.O. Box 5046, 2501 W. 22nd St.; statewide, 1-800-827-1000)
Vet Centers:
Rapid City 57701 (610 Kansas City St., 605-348-0077)
Sioux Falls 57104 (601 S. Cliff Ave., Suite C, 605-332-0856)
Martin 57551 (East Hwy 18, 605-685-1300)
National Cemeteries:
Black Hills (Sturgis 57785, P.O. Box 640, 605-347-3830 or 347-7299)
Fort Meade 57785 (Sturgis 57785; Old Stone Rd.; for information, call 605-347-3830 or 347-7299)
Hot Springs 57747 (VA Medical Center, 605-347-3830 or 347-7299)

TENNESSEE
Medical Centers:
*Memphis 38104 (1030 Jefferson Ave., 901-523-8990)
#*Mountain Home 37684 (Sidney & Lamont St., 423-926-1171)
*Murfreesboro 37129 (3400 Lebanon Pike., 615-893-1360)
Nashville 37212 (1310 24th Ave., South, 615-327-4751)
Clinics:
Arnold AFB 37389 (225 First St., 931-454-6134)
Chattanooga 37411 (150 Debra Rd., Suite 5200, Bldg 6200 East Gate Center, 423-893-6500)

Cookville 38501 (121 S. Dixie Ave., 931-528-2531)

Jonesboro, AR 72401 (223 East Jackson, for information, contact VAMC Memphis)

Knoxville 37923 (9031 Cross Park Dr., 423-545-4592)

Mountain City 37683 (Hospital Drive)

Smithville, MS 38870 (63420 Highway 25 North, for information, contact VAMC Memphis)

Regional Office:

Nashville 37203 (110 9th Ave. South; statewide, 1-800-827-1000)

Vet Centers:

Chattanooga 37411 (951 Eastgate Loop Rd., Bldg. 5700, Suite. 300, 423-855-6570)

Johnson City 37604 (1615A W. Market St., 423-928-8387)

Knoxville 37914 (2817 E. Magnolia Ave., 423-545-4680)

Memphis 38104 (1835 Union, Suite 100, 901-544-0173)

National Cemeteries:

Chattanooga 37404 (1200 Bailey Ave., 423-855-6590)

Knoxville 37917 (939 Tyson St., N.W., for information, call 423-855-6590)

Memphis 38122 (3568 Townes Ave., 901-386-8311)

Mountain Home 37684 (P.O. Box 8, 423-461-7935)

Nashville (Madison 37115-4619, 1420 Gallatin Rd. So., 615-736-2839)

TEXAS

Medical Centers:

*Amarillo 79106 (6010 Amarillo Blvd., West, 806-355-9703)

*Big Spring 79720 (300 Veterans Blvd., 915-263-7361)

Central Texas HC System:
#*Temple 76504 (1901 Veterans Memorial Dr., 800-423-2111)
*Marlin 76661 (1016 Ward St., 254-883-3511)
*Waco 76711 (4800 Memorial Dr., 254-752-6581)

*Houston 77030 (2002 Holcombe Blvd., 713-791-1414)

North Texas HC System:
#*Dallas 75216 (4500 S. Lancaster Rd., 800-849-3597)
#*Bonham 75418 (1201 East Ninth St., 800-924-8387)

South Texas HC System:
*San Antonio 78284 (7400 Merton Minter Blvd., 210-617-5184)
*Kerrville 78028 (3600 Memorial Blvd., 830-792-2514)

Clinics:

Abilene 79606 (6200 Regional Plaza, Suite 1200, 915-695-3252)

Austin 78741 (2901 Montopolis Dr., 512-389-1010)

Beaumont 77701 (3385 Fannin St.)

Beeville 78102 (302 South Hillside Dr., 888-686-6350)

Bishop 78343 (301 W. Main, 888-686-6350)

Bonham (Grayson, Delta, and Lamar Counties, TX, 800-924-8387, ext. 6342 or commercial 903-583-6342)

Brownsville 78520 (394 Military Rd., 888-686-6350); and 78521 (625 E. Price Rd., 88-686-6350)

Brownwood, 76801 (125 S. Park Dr., Suite A, 915-641-0568)

Childress 79201 (Highway 83 North, 940-937-3636)

Cleburne (Johnson and Ellis Counties, 800-924-8387, ext. 6342 or commercial 903-583-6342)

College Station, 77845 (1605 Rock Prairie Rd., Suite 212, 409-680-0361)

100

Corpus Christi 78405 (5283 Old Brownsville Rd., 361-854-7392, ext. 227)

Dallas County 75217 (9202 Elam Rd., Dallas, 800-924-8387, ext. 6342 or commercial 903-583-6342)

Decatur (Wise, Jack, Clay, Archer, Baylor, Young, Throckmorton and Montague Counties, 800-924-8387, ext. 6342 or commercial 903-583-6342)

Del Rio 78840 (913 S. Main St., 888-686-6350)

Denton (Denton, Cooke and Collin Counties, 800-924-8387, ext. 6342 or commercial 903-583-6342)

Eagle Pass 78852 (2525 Loop 431, 888-686-6350)

Eastland (Eastland, Parker, Palo Pinto, Hood, Callahan and Stephens Counties, 800-924-8387, ext. 6342 or commercial 903-583-6342)

El Paso 79930 (5001 N. Piedras St., 915-564-6100)

Fort Worth 76104 (300 W. Rosedale St., 800-443-9672)

Fort Stockton 79735 (Sanderson Hwy., 915-336-8365)

Greenville (Kaufman, Hopkins, Hunt, Rockwall, Titus and Franklin Counties, 800-924-8387, ext. 6342 or commercial 903-583-6342)

Hamilton 76531 (400 N. Brown St., 254-386-3102)

Laredo 78043 (2359 E. Saunders Ave., 956-725-7060, ext. 223)

Lubbock 79410 (4902 34th St., Suite 10, 806-796-7900)

Lufkin 75904 (1301 W. Frank Blvd., 409-637-1342)

McAllen 78503 (2101 S. Colonel Rowe Blvd., 956-618-7103)

Odessa 79761 (419 W. Fourth St., 915-337-1586)

Palestine, 75801 (3215 W. Oak Blvd., Suite 200, 903-723-9006)

San Angelo 76905 (2018 Pulliam, 915-658-6138)

San Antonio 78240 (5788 Eckert Rd., 210-699-2133 or 2125)

San Diego 78527 (102 E. King, Suite 200, 888-686-6350)

South Bexar County 78223 (1055 Ada, San Antonio, 888-686-6350)

Stamford 79553 (1303 Mabee Dr., 915-773-2710)

Stratford 79084 (1220 Purnell St., 806-396-5583)

Tarrant County (, 800-924-8387, ext. 6342 or commercial 903-583-6342)

Texarkana 75503 (2717 Summerhill Rd., 903-793-3371)

Tyler, 75217 (11937 US Hwy 271, 800-924-8387, ext. 6342 or commercial 903-583-6342)

Uvalde 78801 (1042 Garner Field Rd., 888-686-6350)

Victoria 77901 (4206 Retama Circle, 361-572-0006, ext. 225)

Wichita Falls 76301 (1410 Eighth St., 940-723-2373)

Regional Offices:

Houston 77030 (6900 Almeda Rd., statewide, 1-800-827-1000. Serves counties of Angelina, Aransas, Atacosa, Austin, Bandera, Bee, Bexar, Blanco, Brazoria, Brewster, Brooks, Caldwell, Calhoun, Cameron, Chambers, Colorado, Comal, Crockett, DeWitt, Dimitt, Duval, Edwards, Fort Bend, Frio, Galveston, Gillespie, Goliad, Gonzales, Grimes, Guadeloupe, Hardin, Harris, Hays, Hidalgo, Houston, Jackson, Jasper, Jefferson, Jim Hogg, Jim Wells, Karnes, Kendall, Kenedy, Kerr, Kimble, Kinney, Kleberg, LaSalle, Lavaca, Liberty, Live Oak, McCulloch, McMullen, Mason,

Matagorda, Maverlck, Medina,
Menard, Montgomery,
Nacogdoches, Newton, Nueces,
Orange, Pecos, Polk, Real,
Refugio, Sabine, San Augustine,
San Jacinto, San Patricio,
Schleicher, Shelby, Starr, Sutton,
Terrell, Trinity, Tyler, Uvalde, Val
Verde, Victoria, Walker, Waller,
Washington, Webb, Wharton,
Willacy, Wilson, Zapata, Zavala)
Waco 76799 (One Veterans Plaza,
701 Clay; statewide, 1-800-827-
1000; serves the rest of the state)
In Bowie County, the City of
Texarkana is served by Little
Rock, AR, Regional Office, 1-800-
827-1000.

Benefits Offices:
Corpus Christi 78405 (5283 Old
Brownsville Rd., 1-800-827-1000)
Dallas 75242 (Santa Fe Bldg., 1114
Commerce St., 1-800-827-1000)
El Paso 79930 (5001 Piedras Dr., 1-
800-827-1000)
Lubbock 79410 (3208 34th St., Suite
10, 1-800-827-1000)
San Antonio 78240 (5788 Eckert
Rd., 1-800-827-1000)
Tyler 75701 (1700 SSE Loop 323,
Suite 310, 1-800-827-1000)

Vet Centers:
Amarillo 79109 (3414 Olsen Blvd.,
Suite E., 806-354-9779)
Austin 78745 (1110 W. William
Cannon Dr., Suite 301, 512-416-
1314)
Corpus Christi 78411 (4646 Corona,
Suite 110, 361-854-9961)
Dallas 75244 (5232 Forest Lane,
Suite 111, 214-361-5896)
El Paso 79925 (Sky Park II, 6500
Boeing, Suite L-112, 915-772-
5368)
Fort Worth 76104 (1305 W. Magno-
lia, Suite B, 817-921-9095)
Houston 77006 (503 Westheimer,
713-523-0884)

Houston 77024 (701 N. Post Oak
Rd., Suite 102, 713-682-2288)
Laredo 78041 (6020 McPherson Rd.
#1A, 956-723-4680)
Lubbock 79410 (3208 34th St., 806-
792-9782)
McAllen 78504 (801 Nolana Loop,
Suite 115, 956-631-2147)
Midland 79703 (3404 W. Illinois,
Suite 1, 915-697-8222)
San Antonio 78212 (231 W. Cypress
St., 210-472-4025)

National Cemeteries:
Dallas-Fort Worth 75211 (2191
Mountain Creek Parkway, 214-
467-3374, opens in 2000)
Fort Bliss 79906 (5200 Fred Wilson
Rd., P.O. Box 6342, 915-564-
0201)
Fort Sam Houston (San Antonio
78209, 1520 Harry Wurzbach Rd.,
210-820-3891)
Houston 77038 (10410 Veterans
Memorial Dr., 281-447-8686)
Kerrville 78028 (VA Medical Center,
3600 Memorial Blvd.; for informa-
tion, call 210-820-3891)
San Antonio 78202 (517 Paso
Hondo St.; for information, call
210-820-3891)

UTAH
Medical Center:
Salt Lake City 84148 (500 Foothill
Blvd.)
Regional Office:
Salt Lake City 84147 (P.O. Box
11500, Federal Bldg., 125 S. State
St.; statewide, 1-800-827-1000)
Vet Centers:
Provo 84601 (750 North 200 West,
Suite 105, 801-377-1117)
Salt Lake City 84106 (1354 East
3300 South, 801-584-1294)

VERMONT
Medical Center:
White River Junction 05009 (215 N. Main St., 802-295-9363)
Clinics:
Burlington 05401 (1205 North Ave., 802-864-4492)
Bennington 05201 (325 North St., 802 447-6913)
Wilder 05088 (P.O. Box 816, 34 Depot St., 802-295-1311)
Newport 05855 (P.O. Box 724 ,154 Duchess St, 802-334-6744)
St. Johnsbury 05819 (P.O. Box 560 Railroad St., 802-748-3181)
Regional Office:
White River Junction 05009 (215 N. Main St., 802-296-5177, or 1-800-827-1000 from within Vermont only)
Vet Centers:
South Burlington 05403 (359 Dorset St., 802-862-1806)
White River Junction 05001 (Gilman Office Center, Bldg. #2, Holiday Inn Dr., 802-295-2908 or 1-800-649-6603)

VIRGINIA
Medical Centers:
#*Hampton 23667 (100 Emancipation Dr., 757-722-9961)
*Richmond 23249 (1201 Broad Rock Blvd., 804-230-0001)
*Salem 24153 (1970 Roanoke Blvd., 540-982-2463)
Clinics:
Danville 24541 (2811 Riverside Drive, 804-799-1200)
Harrisonburg 22827 (13737 Spotswood Trail, Elkton, 540-298-4666)
Stephens City 22655 (106 Hyde Court, 540-869-0600)
Tazewell 24651 (123 Ben Holt Ave. 540-988-2526))

Regional Offices:
Roanoke 24011 (210 Franklin Rd., S.W.; statewide, 1-800-827-1000)
Northern Virginia counties of Arlington & Fairfax, cities of Alexandria, Fairfax, Falls Church served by Washington, D.C., RO, 1-800-827-1000).
Vet Centers:
Alexandria 22309 (8796 Sacramento Dr., Suite D&E, 703-360-8633)
Norfolk 23517 (2200 Colonial Ave., Suite 3, 757-623-7584)
Richmond 23230 (4202 Fitzhugh Ave., 804-353-8958)
Roanoke 24016 (350 Albemarle Ave., SW, 540-342-9726)
National Cemeteries:
Alexandria 22314 (1450 Wilkes St.; for information, call 703-690-2217)
Balls Bluff (Leesburg 22075, Rte. 7; for information, call 540-825-0027)
City Point (Hopewell 23860, 10th Ave. & Davis St.; for information, call 804-795-2031)
Cold Harbor (Mechanicsville 23111, Rt. 156 North; for information, call 804-795-2031)
Culpeper 22701 (305 U.S. Ave., 540-825-0027)
Danville 24541 (721 Lee St.; for information, call 704-636-2661)
Fort Harrison (Richmond 23231, 8620 Varina Rd.; for information, call 804-795-2031)
Glendale (Richmond 23231, 8301 Willis Church Rd.; for information, call 804-795-2031)
Hampton 23667 (Cemetery Rd. at Marshall Ave., 757-723-7104)
Quantico (Triangle 22172, P.O. Box 10, 18424 Joplin Rd. (Rte. 619), 703-690-2217)
Richmond 23231 (1701 Williamsburg Rd.; for information, call 804-795-2031)

Seven Pines (Sandston 23150, 400
E. Williamsburg Rd.; for informa-
tion, call 804-795-2031)
Staunton 24401 (901 Richmond
Ave.; for information, call
540-825-0027)
Winchester 22601 (401 National
Ave.; for information, call
540-825-0027)

VIRGIN ISLANDS
For information on VA benefits, call
1-800-827-1000.
Vet Centers:
St. Croix 00850 (Box 12, R.R. 02,
Village Mall, #113, 340-778-5553)
St. Thomas 00802 (9800 Buccaneer
Mall, Suite 8, 340-774-6674)

WASHINGTON
Medical Centers:
Puget Sound HC System:
*Seattle 98108 (1660 S.
Columbian Way, 206-762-1010)
#*Tacoma 98493 (9600 Veterans
Dr., S.W., American Lake,
253-582-8440)
*Spokane 99205 (N. 4815 Assembly
St., 509-328-4521)
*Walla Walla 99362 (77 Wainwright
Dr., 509-525-5200)
Clinics:
Tri-Cities (Richland) 99352 (948
Stevens Drive, Suite, C, 509-946-
1020)
Yakima 98902(310 N 5th Ave., 509-
457-2736)
Regional Office:
Seattle 98174 (Federal Bldg., 915
2nd Ave.; statewide, 1-800-827-
1000)
Benefits Office:
Fort Lewis 98433 (Waller Hall Rm.
700, P.O. Box 331153, 253-967-
7106)
Vet Centers:
Bellingham 98226 (3800 Byron Ave.,
Suite 124, 360-733-9226)

Seattle 98121 (2030 9th Ave., Suite
210, 206-553-2706)
Spokane 99201 (W. 1708 Mission
Ave., 509-327-0274)
Tacoma 98409 (4916 Center St.,
Suite E, 253-565-7038)
Toppenish 98498 (219 S. Toppenish
Ave.)
Yakima 98901 (310 N. 5th Ave., 509-
457-2736)
National Cemetery:
Tahoma (Kent 98042-4868, 18600
S.E. 240th St., 425-413-9614)

WEST VIRGINIA
Medical Center:
*Beckley 25801 (200 Veterans Ave.,
304-255-2121)
Clarksburg 26301 (1 Medical Center
Dr., 304-623-3461)
Huntington 25704 (1540 Spring
Valley Dr., 304-429-6741)
#*Martinsburg 25401 (Route 9,
304-263-0811 or 1-800-817-3807)
Clinics:
Franklin 26807 (305 North Main St.,
304-358-2355)
Gassaway 26624 (707 Elk Street,
304-623-3461, ext. 3332)
Parkersburg 26101 (912 Market
Street, 304-422-5114)
Parsons 26287 (2061/2 Spruce
Street, 304-478-2219)
Petersburg 26847 (Route 55 West,
304-257-1026)
Regional Office:
Huntington 25701 (640 Fourth Ave.,
statewide, 1-800-827-1000;
counties of Brooke, Hancock,
Marshall, Ohio, served by
Pittsburgh, Pa., RO)
Vet Centers:
Beckley 25801 (101 Ellison Ave.,
304-252-8220)
Charleston 25302 (512 Washington
St. West, 304-343-3825)
Huntington 25701 (1005 6th Ave.,
304-523-8387)

104

#Martinsburg 25401 (105 S. Spring St., 304-263-6776)
Morgantown 26505 (1191F Pineview Dr., 304-285-4001)
Princeton 24740 (905 Mercer St., 304-425-5653)
Wheeling 26003 (1206 Chapline St., 304-232-0587)

National Cemeteries:
Grafton 26354 (431 Walnut St.; for information, call 304-265-2044)
West Virginia (Grafton 26354, Rt. 2, Box 127, 304-265-2044)

WISCONSIN
Medical Centers:
Madison 53705 (2500 Overlook Terrace, 608-256-1901)
#*Milwaukee 53295 (5000 W. National Ave., 414-384-2000)
*Tomah 54660 (500 E. Veterans St., 608-372-3971)

Clinics:
Appleton 54914 (10 Tri-Park Way, 920-831-0070)
Baraboo 53913 (626 14th St., 608-280-7078)
Beaver Dam 53916 (208 LaCrosse St., 608-280-7078)
Chippewa Falls 54729 (2503 County Rd. I, 715-720-3780)
Cleveland 53015 (1205 North Ave., 920-693-3750)
Edgerton 53534 (92 E. Hwy. 59, 608-280-7078)
LaCrosse 54601-3200 (300 4th St. N., 2nd Floor, 608-784-3886)
Loyal 54446 (141 North Main St.)
Rhinelander 54501 (5 W. Frederick, 715-362-4080)
Superior 54880 (3520 Tower Ave., 715-392-9711)
Union Grove 53182 (21425 Spring St., 414-878-7820)
Wausau 54401 (995 Campus Dr., 715-675-3391)

Regional Office:
Milwaukee 53295 (5000 W. National Ave., Bldg. 6; statewide, 1-800-827-1000)

Vet Centers:
Madison 53703 (147 S. Butler St., 608-264-5342)
Milwaukee 53218 (5401 N. 76th St., 414-536-1301)

National Cemetery:
Wood (Milwaukee 53295-4000, 5000 W. National Ave., Bldg. 1301, 414-382-5300)

WYOMING
Medical Centers
*Cheyenne 82001 (2360 E. Pershing Blvd., 307-778-7550)
*Sheridan 82801 (1898 Fort Rd., 307-672-3473)

Clinic:
Ft. Collins 80524 (1100 Poudre River Dr., 970-224-1550)

Benefits Office:
Cheyenne 82001 (2360 E. Pershing Blvd.; statewide, 1-800-827-1000)

Vet Centers:
Casper 82601 (111 S. Jefferson, 307-261-5355)
Cheyenne 82001 (3130 Henderson Dr., 307-778-7370)

The VA Online

The Department of Veterans Affairs (VA) Web site is a worldwide resource that provides information on VA programs, veterans benefits, VA facilities worldwide, and VA medical automation software. Made available on September 1994, the site serves several major constituencies, including the veteran and his or her dependents, Veterans Service Organizations, the military, the general public, and VA employees around the world. These documents are easily accessible and richly linked from their table of contents, as well as searchable by keyword.

Internet mail is also available, which allows veterans to make specific inquiries and receive official responses from VA staff. In addition to providing the text of this book (available as PDFs), press releases and announcements of interest to veterans, a listing of current job opportunities with the VA and many of the most requested benefit application and information forms are now available to you.

The VA Web site can be accessed at www.va.gov.

Forms Online

When you access the Veterans Benefits Administration Web site at http://www.va.gov/forms/, you can follow hyperlinks to many online forms. Note that many of the forms have multiple pages. To complete a form, you need to download **all** its pages. These forms are in the PDF format, requiring Adobe Acrobat Reader. If you experience difficulty reading or interpreting either the form or instructions, please call your local VA office or the VA toll free number 1-800-827-1000.

The following form prefixes denote functional areas of responsibility:

20 - Forms that affect more than one VBA area
21 - Compensation and Pension
22 - Education
24 - Finance / Budget
26 - Loan Guaranty
28 - Vocational Rehabilitation
29 - Insurance
Other forms under the control of VBA

Veterans Benefits Administration Forms

20-5655 Financial Status Report (2 pages)

Compensation and Pension Forms

21-0304 Application for Spina Bifida Benefits (1 page)
21-0514-1 Parent's DIC Eligibility Verification Report (2 pages)

21-526	Veteran's Application for Compensation or Pension (11 pages) (Attachment VA Form 21-4142, Authorization and Consent To Release Information To The Department of Veterans Affairs (VA), is 2 pages)
21-527	Income-Net Worth And Employment Statement (6 pages)
21-530*	Application For Burial Benefits (Under 38 U.S.C. Chapter 23) (4 pages)
21-534	Application for Dependency and Indemnity Compensation, Death Pension and Accrued Benefits by a Surviving Spouse or Child (Including Death Compensation if Applicable) (12 pages)
21-535	Application for Dependency and Indemnity Compensation by Parent(s) (8 pages; 1-4 are instructions; 5-7 are form; page 8 is SSA form 24)
21-601	Application For Reimbursement From Accrued Amounts Due A Deceased Beneficiary (2 pages)
21-674	Request For Approval of School Attendance (4 pages)
21-686c	Declaration of Status of Dependents (2 pages)
21-2008	Application For United States Flag For Burial Purposes (3 pages)
21-4138	Statement in Support of Claim (1 page)
21-4142	Authorization And Consent To Release Information To The Department of Veterans Affairs (VA) (2 pages)
21-4703	Fiduciary Agreement (3 pages)
21-6753	Original Or Amended Dependency and Indemnity Compensation Award (2 pages)
21-8416	Medical Expense Report (2 pages)
21-8678	Application For Annual Clothing Allowance (1 page)
21-8940	Veteran's Application For Increased Compensation Based On Unemployability (2 pages)

Education Forms

22-1990	Application for VA Education Benefits (8 pages)
22-1990t	Application and Enrollment Certification For Individualized Tutorial Assistance (38 U.S.C. Chapters 30, 32 or 35 and 10 U.S.C. Chapter 1606) (2 pages)
22-1995	Request For Change of Program or Place of Training (2 pages)
22-1999b	Notice of Change in Student Status (4 pages)
22-5490	Application For Survivors' and Dependents' Educational Assistance (6 pages)
22-5495	Request for Change of Program or Place of Training Survivors' and Dependents' Educational Assistance (6 pages)

22-6553c   Monthly Certification Of Flight Training (2 pages)

22-8690   Time Record (Work-Study Program) (2 pages)

22-8873   Supplemental Information For Change of Program Or Reenrollment After Unsatisfactory Attendance, Conduct or Progress (2 pages)

Finance Forms

24-0296   Direct Deposit Enrollment (1 page)

24-5281   Application For Refund of Education Contributions (VEAP, Chapter 32, Title 38, U.S.C.) (1 page)

Loan Guaranty Forms

26-0286   VA Loan Summary Sheet (8 1/2 x 14) (2 pages)

26-0503   Federal Collection Policy Notice (1 page)

26-1802a   HUD/VA Addendum to Uniform Residential Loan Application (5 pages)

26-1814   Batch Transmittal - Loan Code Sheet (1 page)

26-1817   Request For Determination Of Loan Guaranty Eligibility - Unremarried Surviving Spouses (1 page)

26-1839   Compliance Inspection Report (8 1/2" x 14") (10 pages)

26-1847*   Request For Postponement Of Offsite Or Exterior Onsite Improvements - Home Loan (1 page)

26-1852   Description of Materials (6 pages) (NOTE: This form is the same as the Housing and Urban Development/HUD- 92005)

26-1880   Request For A Certificate of Eligibility For VA Home Loan Benefits (2 pages)

26-6382   Statement of Purchaser Or Owner Assuming Seller's Loan (2 pages)

26-6393   Loan Analysis (8 1/2 x 14) (1 page)

26-6684   Statement of Fee Appraisers or Compliance Inspectors (2 pages)

26-6705   Offer to Purchase and Contract of Sale (8 1/2 x 14) (2 pages)

26-6705b   Credit Statement of Prospective Purchaser (8 1/2 x 14) (2 pages)

26-6807   Financial Statement (8 1/2 x 14) (2 pages)

26-8736a   NonSupervised Lender's Nomination and Recommendation of Credit Underwriter (1 page)

26-8812   VA Equal Opportunity Lender Certification (2 pages)

26-8937   Verification of VA Benefit-Related Indebtedness (1 page)

Vocational Rehabilitation and Employment Forms

28-1900   Disabled Veterans Application For Vocational Rehabilitation (2 pages)

28-1902   Counseling Record - Personal Information (2 pages)

28-1902n	Counseling Record - Narrative Report (Supplemental Sheet) (2 pages)
28-8872	Rehabilitation Plan (2 pages)
28-8872a	Rehabilitation Plan - Continuation Sheet (2 pages)
28-8890	Important Information About Rehabilitation Benefits (2 pages)

Insurance Forms

29-336	Designation of Beneficiary - Government Life Insurance (2 pages)
29-1546	Application For Cash Surrender Value / Application For Policy Loan (2 pages)
29-4125	Claim For One Sum Payment (1 page)
29-4364*	Application For Service-Disabled Insurance - (2 pages)

Forms Used by VBA

DD 149	Application for Correction of Military Record Under the Provisions of Title 10, U.S. Code, Section 1552 (2 pages)(This is a Department of Defense form)
DD 293	Application for the Review of Discharge OR Dismissal From the Armed Forces of the United States (4 pages)(This is a Department of Defense form)
SF 15	Application for 10-Point Veteran's Preference (This is not a VA Form) (Link to Office of Personnel Management - (2 pages))
SF 180	Request Pertaining To Military Records - (This is not a VA Form) (Link to the National Personnel & Military Records Centers and Related Forms/Also, FAQ about military and genealogy)
SGLV8283	Claim For Death Benefits - Form returned to Office of Servicemembers' Group Life Insurance (2 pages)
SGLV8285	Request For Insurance - (Servicemembers' Group Life Insurance) (2 pages)
SGLV8286	Servicemembers' Group Life Insurance Election and Certificate (8 pages)
SGLV8714	Application For Veterans' Group Life Insurance - (5 pages)
VAF8	Certification of Appeal - (1 page)
VAF9	Appeal to Board of Veterans' Appeals (5 pages)
VAF4107	Notice of Procedural And Appellate Rights (1 page)

Other Forms Available Online

DOD Forms

Dept. of Defense forms page
http://web1.whs.osd.mil/ICDHOME/DDEFORMS.HTM

GSA Forms
General Services Administration forms page
http://www.gsa.gov/forms/forms.htm

HUD Forms
Housing and Urban Development Agency Forms
http://www.hudclips.org/sub_nonhud/html/forms.htm

OPM Forms
Office of Personnel Management Forms
http://www.opm.gov/forms/html/opm.htm

VETS-100 Report Form
Department of Labor
http://vets100.cudenver.edu/

VHA Forms
968 VHA forms used by VAMCs
http://www.va.gov/forms/medical/SearchList.asp

Frequently Asked Questions: Online Answers

Before you contact a VA office with your question, check these Frequently Asked Questions (FAQ). Chances are, someone else has asked it.

You can find answers to the following questions online at http://www.va.gov/customer/consumer.htm#faq. Just follow the hyperlinks to the answers!

How can I find information regarding Veterans Service Organizations in my area?

I have WebTV, why can't I access certain information on the VA site with the WebTV interface?

How can I find information regarding VA Health Care Services?

How do I find out the status of my claim?

How do I apply for compensation benefits?

How do I find the email address of a VA employee?

What medals, commendations, or awards did I (or another veteran) receive while in military service?

How Can I Upgrade My Military Discharge?

How do I see my records or the records of a family member who is a veteran?

How do I obtain a copy of my Report of Separation from Active Duty (DD-214)?

How do I find out about VA-acquired properties for sale?

How do I update my VA records or change my address?

Is it true that Congress has recently passed a bill which entitles veterans and service persons to a dividend based upon their prior years of service?

How do I find a veteran, a servicemate, or members of my military unit?

How do I contact the Secretary? Does he have an e-mail address?

How can I get a job at VA?

What are my employment rights as a veteran? Do I get preference for Federal jobs?

Who do I talk to if I'm being discriminated against on the job because I'm a veteran?

Does VA employ veterans with disabilities?

Where Can I Get Information on Agent Orange?

Where can I get a VA form?

What programs are available for women veterans?

Doesn't the Lincoln quotation ignore the fact that there are two million women veterans who deserve VA care?

How can I order a headstone or marker for a deceased veteran?

What other burial benefits are available?

How can I volunteer to help veterans?

How do I locate and learn about U.S. Veterans memorials?

May I use the stylized VA logo or the "official" VA seal on my Web site?

May I link to WWW.VA.GOV? How may I get a link for my web page on WWW.VA.GOV?

How does my VA facility or program get a home page on WWW.VA.GOV?

VA Internet Server

Check the VA Web site for updates to this listing.

Programs with Internet Servers

The Chronic Pain Rehabilitation Program at the James A. Haley Veterans Hospital; Tampa, FL

GRECCs (Geriatric Research, Education and Clinical Centers)

GRECC at Salt Lake City, UT VAMC http://slcgrecc.med.utah.edu/saltlake

GRECC at Gainesville, FL VAMC http://www.med.ufl.edu/pharm/facdata/GRECC/

Management Science Group of the Chief Information Officer, Veterans Health Administration http://world.std.com/~mgtsci

Rehabilitation Research and Development Center at Palo Alto

Quality Enhancement Research Initiative (QUERI) for Spinal Cord Injury

San Diego VAMC Research Service

VA Debt Management Center, Ft. Snelling, MN

VA Online - Research names on the Vietnam Veterans Memorial with Telnet to VA Online (If you do not have Telnet access, you may use your modem to call 1-800-US1-VETS at up to 28.8 kbps at 8-N-1 modem setting). Be sure to take the MRI tutorial. You can also access VA Online by FTP at vaonline.va.gov.

VA Greenhouse (Veterans at the Bedford VAMC, Bedford, Ma)

The VA Regional Office and Insurance Center

The Veterans Affairs Hispanic Association (VAHA) is a nonprofit organization established in the Department of Veterans Affairs Central Office by VA employees to promote awareness of Hispanic culture and contributions by Hispanics to American social, community and economic life.

The Vocational Rehabilitation & Counseling Division, Wichita, KS, provides courteous, quality and professional services designed to assist eligible veterans, service members, and dependents to attain their maximum vocational potential.

Learn about opportunities to sell products and services to the VA with the VA Vendor BBS. Use your modem to call 1-800-SELL-2-VA at 8-N-1 modem setting (sorry, no Telnet access yet).

VISNs with Internet Servers

VISN 1 - New England Health Care System

VISN 2 - VA Health Care Network Upstate New York

VISN 3 - VA New York/New Jersey Health Care System

VISN 4 - VA Stars & Stripes Health Care Network

VISN 5 - VA Capitol Network

VISN 6 - VA Mid-Atlantic Network

VISN 7 - Atlanta Network

VISN 8 - Florida

VISN 9 - Mid-South Health Care Network

VISN 10 - VA Health Care System of Ohio

VISN 11 - MI, Northern IN, Central IL, and Toledo, OH

VISN 12 - Great Lakes Health Care System

VISN 13 - VA Upper Midwest Network

VISN 14 - Central Plains Network

VISN 15 - VA Heartland Network

VISN 16 - OK, AR, LA, MS, and parts of TX, MO, AL and FL

VISN 17 - VA Heart of Texas Health Care Network

VISN 18 - Southwest Network of AZ, NM, West TX

VISN 19 - VA Rocky Mountain Network

VISN 20 - Northwest Network

VISN 21 - VA Sierra Pacific Network

VISN 22 - VA Desert Pacific Health Care Network

Facilities with Internet Servers

Ann Arbor VAMC

Atlanta VA Regional Office

Austin Automation Center

Boston VA Regional Office

Boston VAMC

Brockton/WestRoxbury VAMC

Clarksburg VAMC

Cleveland VAMC

Coatesville VAMC Veterans Industries Compensated Work Therapy Program

Financial Service Center, Texas

Gainesville, FL, USA., Magnetic Resonance Imaging (MRI) Server at the VA
Medical Center

Maryland Health Care System

Milwaukee VAMC

Murfreesboro VAMC

Northern California Health Care System

Phoenix VA Regional Office

Southern Arizona VA Healthcare System

South Texas Healthcare System

Washington, D.C. VAMC

Washington State Dept. of Veterans Affairs Homepage

Wichita VA Regional Office

Contractors with Internet Servers

Advanced Management Technology, Incorporated (A.M.T.I.)

EDS, Inc.

The Lake Area Health Education Center (LAHEC) is a non-profit organization committed to the highest quality and lowest cost continuing
education possible. Working with its membership, the Department of
Veterans Affairs Health Care System, and other individuals or organizations, LAHEC seeks to improve the quality of health care by facilitating
the continuing education of health manpower. Send your email to
G.LAHEC@erie.va.gov -or- LAHEC@erie.net.

Performax3 - interactive computer-based programs

114

Veteran's Preference

For detailed information pertaining to the employment of veterans in Federal jobs, check out the Office of Personnel Management's *Vet Guide* at http://www.opm.gov/veterans/html/vetguide.htm#TOP and the *VetsInfo Guide* at http://www.opm.gov/veterans/html/vetsinfo.htm.

Since the time of the Civil War, Veterans of the Armed Forces have been given some degree of preference in appointments to Federal jobs. Recognizing that sacrifices are made by those serving in the Armed Forces, Congress enacted laws to prevent veterans seeking Federal employment from being penalized because of the time spent in military service

By law, veterans who are disabled or who served on active duty in the Armed Forces during certain specified time periods or in military campaigns are entitled to preference over nonveterans both in hiring from competitive lists of eligibles and in retention during reductions in force.

Preference does not have as its goal the placement of a veteran in every vacant Federal job; this would be incompatible with the merit principle of public employment. Nor does it apply to promotions or other in-service actions. However, preference does provide a uniform method by which special consideration is given to qualified veterans seeking Federal employment.

Preference applies in hiring from civil service examinations, for most excepted service jobs, and when agencies make temporary appointments or use direct hire and delegated examining authorities from the U. S. Office of Personnel Management.

General Requirements for Preference

To be entitled to preference, a veteran must meet the eligibility requirements in section 2108 of title 5, United States Code. This means that:

An honorable or general discharge is necessary.

♦ Military retirees at the rank of major, lieutenant commander, or higher are not eligible for preference unless they are disabled veterans.

♦ Guard and Reserve active duty for training purposes does not qualify for preference.

♦ When applying for Federal jobs, eligible veterans should claim preference on their application or resume. Applicants claiming 10-point preference must complete form SF-15, Application for 10-Point Veteran Preference.

Note that the Application for 10-Point Veteran Preference is available in PDF format at http://www.opm.gov/forms/pdfimage/sf0015.pdf.

115

Types of Preference

5-Point Preference

Five points are added to the passing examination score of a veteran who served:

♦ During the period December 7, 1941, to July 1, 1955; or

♦ For more than 180 consecutive days, any part of which occurred after January 31, 1955, and before October 15, 1976; or

♦ During the Gulf War from August 2, 1990 through January 2, 1992; or

♦ In a campaign or expedition for which a campaign medal has been authorized, including El Salvador, Grenada, Haiti, Lebanon, Panama, Somalia, Southwest Asia, and Bosnia.

Medal holders and Gulf War veterans who enlisted after September 7, 1980, or entered on active duty on or after October 14, 1982, must have served continuously for 24 months or the full period called or ordered to active duty. The service requirement does not apply to veterans with compensable service-connected disabilities, or to veterans separated for disability in the line of duty, or for hardship.

10-Point Preference

Ten points are added to the passing examination score of:

♦ A veteran who served at any time and who (1) has a present service-connected disability or (2) is receiving compensation, disability retirement benefits, or pension from the military or the Department of Veterans Affairs. Individuals who received a Purple Heart qualify as disabled veterans.

♦ An unmarried spouse of certain deceased veterans, a spouse of a veteran unable to work because of a service-connected disability, and

♦ A mother of a veteran who died in service or who is permanently and totally disabled.

Preference in Examination

Veterans meeting the criteria for preference and who are found eligible (achieve a score of 70 or higher either by a written examination or an evaluation of their experience and education) have 5 or 10 points added to their numerical ratings depending on the nature of their preference. For scientific and professional positions in grade GS-9 or higher, names of all eligibles are listed in order of ratings, augmented by veteran preference, if any. For all other positions, the names of 10-point preference eligibles who have a compensable, service-connected disability of 10 percent or more are placed ahead of the names of all other eligibles on a given register. The names of other 10-point preference eligibles, 5-point preference eligibles, and non-veterans are listed in order of their numerical ratings.

Entitlement to veterans' preference does not guarantee a job. There are many ways an agency can fill a vacancy other than by appointment from a list of eligibles.

Filing Applications After Examinations Have Been Closed

A 10-point preference eligible may file an application at any time for any positions for which a nontemporary appointment has been made from a competitive list of eligibles within the past 3 years.

In addition, a person who is unable to file for an open competitive examination because of military service may file after the closing date.

In either of the above situations, the veteran should contact the agency that announced the position for further information.

Positions for Preference Eligibles Only

Certain examinations are open only to preference eligibles as long as such applicants are available. These are custodian, guard, elevator operator and messenger. This limitation applies only to initial employment and does not usually prevent an agency from filling one of these jobs by other means.

Special Complaint Procedures for Veterans

Veterans who believe that they have not been accorded the preference to which they are entitled may file a complaint under a U.S. Department of Labor and U.S. Office of Personnel Management Memorandum of Understanding (refer to Federal Employment Info Line Sheet EI-44, Special Complaint Procedures for Veterans).

The Department of Labor's Office of the Assistant Secretary for Policy and Veterans' Employment and Training Service developed an "expert system" to help veterans receive the preferences to which they are entitled. Two versions of this system are currently available, both of which, help the veterans determine the type of preference to which they are entitled, the benefits associated with the preference and the steps necessary to file a complaint due to the failure of a Federal Agency to provide those benefits. The Internet address for the veterans' preference program is http://www.dol.gov/dol/vets/public/programs/programs/preference/main.htm (State Employment Service Offices have veteran representatives available to assist veterans in gaining access to this information.)

The History of Veterans Preference

Preference Before the Civil War

The use of preference in Federal appointments extends back to the days of the Revolutionary War. Though no legal basis existed to govern the treatment of war veterans, certain soldiers were rewarded for their service by the Federal government. Early forms of preference were often based on European models and featured the use of pensions, bonuses for service, disability allowance, and hospitalization for injuries incurred while in uniform, as rewards for service to one's country. It wasn't until the heyday of the spoils system, however, that appointments to Federal positions as a reward for military service become a popular practice. These appointments, however, were usually reserved for ex-officers, and not for the rank and file soldier.

Civil War to the end of World War I

Towards the end of the Civil War, congress passed the first significant veterans' preference legislation. This act provided that,

> "Persons honorably discharged from the military or naval service by reason of disability resulting from wounds or sickness incurred in the line of duty shall be preferred for appointments to civil offices, provided they are found to possess the business capacity necessary for the proper discharge of the duties of such offices."

Under this legislation, preference in appointments was limited to disabled veterans who were otherwise qualified for the work to be performed. This 1865 law stood as the basic preference legislation until the end of World War I.

Along the way, however, several modifications were made to the 1865 legislation. An amendment in 1871 contained the first instance of "suitability" requirements for job seeking veterans. The language read as follows,

> "The President is authorized to prescribe such regulations for the admission of persons into the civil service of the United States as may best promote the efficiency thereof, and ascertain the fitness of each candidate in respect to age, health, character, knowledge, and ability for the branch of service into which he seeks to enter, and for this purpose he may employ suitable persons to conduct such inquiries, and may prescribe their duties, and establish regulations for the conduct of persons who may receive appointment in the civil service."

In 1876, another Congressional amendment gave preference for RIF retention to veterans, their widows, and their orphans. This amendment marked the introduction of the use of preference as RIF protection. It provided:

> "That in making any reduction in force in any of the executive departments the head of such department shall retain those persons who

may be equally qualified who have been honorably discharged from the military or naval service of the United States and the widows and orphans of deceased soldiers and sailors."

Determination of the "equal qualifications" of a person entitled to preference under this law was left to the appointing officer.

In 1888, a Civil Service Commission regulation gave absolute preference to all disabled veterans over all other eligibles. In other words, they would qualify with a score of 65, when the minimum passing score for everyone else was a 70, and would be placed at the top of the certification list.

A year later, President Harrison issued an Executive Order allowing honorably discharged veterans who were former Federal employees to be reinstated without time limit. This was the first appearance of reinstatement eligibility as applied to veterans. In 1892, reinstatement rights were extended to the widows and orphans of veterans. The reinstatement provision was the last significant addition to preference legislation until 1919.

Preference Between the World Wars

The first major expansion of Veterans' Preference benefits occurred in 1919 in the form of the Census Act. This act, amended shortly thereafter by the Deficiency Act of 1919 granted preference to all honorably discharged veterans, their widows, and the wives of injured veterans. An excerpt reads as follows:

> "That hereafter in making appointments to clerical and other positions in the executive branch of the Government, in the District of Columbia or elsewhere preference shall be given to honorably discharged soldiers, sailors, and marines, and widows of such, and to the wives of injured soldiers, sailors, and marines, who themselves are not qualified, but whose wives are qualified to hold such positions."

This act is significant for two reasons: it no longer emphasized a service-connected disability as the primary basis for granting veterans' preference, and it introduced the concept of spousal preference in the appointing process. This act redefined eligible veterans to mean all persons who served in an active military capacity and were honorably discharged, whether the service was in wartime or peacetime. Added were their widows and the wives of those too disabled to qualify for government employment. This act remained the basic Federal law for appointment preference until June 27, 1944, when the Veterans' Preference Act of 1944 was enacted.

Two significant modifications were made to the 1919 Act. In 1923, an Executive Order was created which added a 10-points to the score of disabled veterans and added 5-points to the scores of non-disabled veterans. This was the first time the points were added to the examination scores in the appointing process. Under this Executive Order, however, veterans were no longer placed at the top of the certification lists. In 1929, another executive order restored the placement of 10-point disabled veterans to the top of certification lists.

In 1938, a Civil Service Commission rule required that the decision by an appointing official to pass over a veteran and select a non-veteran for appointment be subject to review by the commission. Language regarding the pass-over of eligible veterans existed in earlier executive orders, but these early versions only required that the CSC be notified if a pass-over occurred. The 1938 rule strengthened this requirement and marked the first time that the Commission could overturn the pass-over if it did not regard the reasons as being adequate.

Veterans' Preference Act of 1944

Veterans' preference, as it exists today, derives from the Veterans' Preference Act of 1944. This act, to a large extent, resulted from the veterans organizations' desire to elevate the existing Executive and regulatory orders governing preference to the level of National policy. With a victorious end to World War II clearly in sight, both Congress and the Administration were sympathetic to the veterans organizations' objective. In his endorsement of the legislation, President Roosevelt wrote,

> "I believe that the Federal Government, functioning in its capacity as an employer, should take the lead in assuring those who are in the armed forces that when they return special consideration will be given to them in their efforts to obtain employment. It is absolutely impossible to take millions of our young men out of their normal pursuits for the purpose of fighting to preserve the Nation, and then expect them to resume their normal activities without having any special consideration shown them."

The act, in essence, was a consolidation of the various preference provision already in effect by the various Executive Orders and CSC regulations. It went a step further by broadening and strengthening existing veterans' preference rules by giving them legislative sanction. Thus, the Executive Branch could no longer change the provisions of veterans' preference. Any changes must now be sought through legislation. In addition, the act made clear that preference was a to be a reward for patriotic duties by a grateful country willing to recognize the sacrifices of its servicemen when peace comes. The Act would help ensure that veterans obtain or regain an economic position they otherwise would have attained had they not served in the armed forces.

The Veterans preference Act of 1944 defined to whom and under what circumstances preference would be granted. It provided that Preference be given in competitive examinations, in appointments to positions in the Federal service, in reinstatement to positions, in reemployment, and in retention during reductions in force. Preference would apply to civilian positions - permanent or temporary - in all departments, agencies, bureaus, administrations, establishments, and projects of the Federal Government, and in the civil service of the District of Columbia. Further, the law provided that preference apply to positions in the classified civil service (now the competitive service), the unclassified civil service (positions excepted from the competitive service), and in any temporary or emergency establishment, agency, bureau, administration, project and department created by acts of Congress or Presidential Executive order. The legislative and judicial branches of the Government, as well as positions in the executive branch, which are required to be confirmed by the Senate, except Postmaster-ships, in the first-, second-, and third-class post offices were exempt from the Act.

The Act originally granted preference to non-disabled veterans, disabled veterans, wives of disabled veterans, and the widows of disabled veterans. These were substantially the same groups granted preference under previous laws and regulations with two exceptions. Non-disabled veterans whose only service was performed during peacetime and the wives of non-service-connected disabled veterans over 55 years of age were no longer eligible for preference.

Veterans' Preference Since 1944

In 1948, the Veterans Preference Act of 1944 was amended to include the mothers of veterans. Mother preference was granted to certain widowed, or divorced or legally separated mothers of veterans (men and women) who (a) died under honorable conditions while on active duty in any branch of the armed forces of the United States in wartime or in peacetime campaigns or expeditions for which campaign badges or service medals have been authorized; or (b) have permanent and total service-connected disabilities which disqualify them for civil service appointment to positions along the general line of their usual occupations. In the case of such widowed mothers, preference was granted provided they were widowed at the time of death or disability of the veteran and had not remarried. The divorced or legally separated mothers were granted preference only if the veteran was the mother's only child. This provision was later amended in 1950 to allow preference to mothers who are living with their husbands but whose husbands are totally and permanently disabled.

In 1952, a bill was passed granting preference benefits to those honorably separated veterans who served on active duty in any branch of the armed forces of the United States during the period beginning April 28, 1952 and ending July 1, 1955 (the period after the termination of the state of war between the United States and the Government of Japan during which persons could be inducted under existing law for training and service in the armed forces). The bill also extended preference to the widows and mothers of such veterans.

The Vietnam conflict in the 1960s resulted in several modifications of the VP law of 1944. In 1966, legislation was passed which granted peace-time preference for Vietnam-era vets who served on active duty for more that 180 consecutive days between January 31 1955 and Oct 10, 1976; National guard and reserve service was excluded from this legislation.

In 1967 legislation was passed which expanded preference to all veterans who served on active duty for more than 180 days (no requirement to serve during war, campaign, or conflict) between January 31, 1955 and October 10, 1976. As with the previous year's law, National guard and reserve service was not included in this expansion.

The end of the Vietnam conflict brought with it yet another law, passed in 1976. This law put added restrictions on veterans whose service begins after October 14, 1976. For post-Vietnam era veterans, preference was granted only if theses veterans became disabled, or served in a declared war, a campaign, or expedition. This legislation was the result of the conclusion of the Vietnam conflict and its draft, the Department of Defenses' desire to build a career military service, and veterans organizations' concern that preference was not appropriate for purely peacetime service.

The Civil Service reform act of 1978 created new benefits for veterans with a 30 percent or more disability. It also gave veterans extra protection in hiring and retention. Under this act, preference was no longer granted to nondisabled veterans who retired at the rank of major or above.

In 1988, a law was passed that required the Department of Labor to report agencies' violations of veterans' preference and failure to list vacancies with State employment services to the Office of Personnel Management for enforcement.

The last major legislation affecting veterans' preference occurred in the form of the Defense Appropriations act of 1997. Under this legislation, preference was accorded to anyone who served on active duty during the Gulf War period (August 2, 1990 through January 2, 1992). This law also granted preference to certain service members who earned campaign medals for service in Bosnia and Herzegovina in support of Operation Joint Endeavor (November 20, 1995 through December 20, 1996) or Operation Joint Guard (December 20, 1996 through a date designated by the Secretary of Defense).

Time line of Veterans' Preference in the Federal Civil Service

1865   First veterans' preference (VP) in appointment law; for Union veterans separated for wounds or illnesses. Vets must have been honorably discharged and qualified for job.

1876   First VP in reduction in force (RIF) law

1919	After World War I, law grants VP to all honorably discharged veterans, their widows, and the spouses of veterans too disabled to work
1923	To distinguish between the preference and granted by the 1865 and 1919 laws, an Executive Order grants disabled vets 10 points and other vets 5 points, to be added to their individual numerical ratings in examinations (pt system first introduced)
1929	Executive Order places disabled vets at the top of examination lists of eligibles and continues 10 extra points
1944	Veterans' Preference Act incorporates 1865, 1876, and 1919 laws, plus Executive Orders for extra points, passover protection, and rule of three. Continues to be cornerstone of veterans' civil service legislation today (applied preference to active duty service during war, expedition, or campaign for which badge was authorized, must be separated under hon cond, rule of three)
1952	Amendment extended 1944 law to include active duty service from 4/28/52 - 7/1/55 Korean War
1966	Peacetime preference for Vietnam-era vets added active duty for >180 consecutive days between Jan 31 1955 and Oct 10, 1976; guard and reserve service not included
1967	Expanded 1967 act to all vets who served on active duty for >180 days (no req to serve during war, campaign, or conflict) between Jan 31, 1955 and Oct 10, 1976 (guard and reserve service not included)
1968	Executive Order creates Veterans' Transitional Appointment, a new way for Vietnam-era veterans to enter Federal service without public examination. Forerunner of Veterans Readjustment Appointment (VRA)
1974	VRA enacted into law
1976	By law, veterans whose service begins after October 14, 1976 are granted preference only if they become disabled, or serve in a declared war, a campaign, or expedition. (This resulted from the end of the Vietnam conflict and draft, Department of Defenses desire to build a career military service, and veterans' groups concern that preference was not appropriate for purely peace-time service.)
1978	Civil Service reform act creates new benefits for 30 percent or more disabled veterans; special appointing authority, and extra protection in hiring and retention. Preference ends for nondisabled retired majors and above. Efforts to broaden rule of three and make exceptions to numerical ratings in examinations defeated by veterans' groups

1988	Law requires Dept. of Labor to report agencies' violations of veterans' preference and failure to list vacancies with State employment services to OPM for enforcement
1990	VRA law amended to include post-Vietnam-era veterans, but end coverage of most Vietnam-era veterans
1992	VRA law revised to restore eligibility to Vietnam-era veterans
1997	Defense Appropriations Act grants preference to gulf war veterans and certain campaign medal holders in Bosnia (included guard or reserve service if for other than training)
1999	The Veterans Employment Opportunities Act of 1998 as amended by Section 511 of the Veterans Millennium Health Care Act (Pub. Law 106-117) of November 30, 1999, provides that agencies must allow eligible veterans to apply for positions announced under merit promotion procedures when the agency is recruiting from outside its own workforce.
2000	The National Defense Authorization Act of Fiscal Year 2000 (Public Law 106-65) repeals the reductions in retired or retainer pay previously required of retired members of a uniformed service who are employed in a civilian office or position of the U.S. Government. This repeal is effective retroactively to October 1, 1999.

Index

Other fine titles available from JIST!
See below for toll-free order number!

The Federal Resume Guidebook,
Second Edition
By Kathryn Kraemer Troutman

Revised to reflect the latest federal processes and requirements.

✔ Teaches readers the differences between federal and private industry resumes and how to convert SF-171's into effective federal resumes.

✔ Guidelines for submitting a scannable resume and maximizing scanner "hits."

Careers/Government • Softcover • © 1999, 8.5 x 11, 418 pp. • 1-56370-545-1 • $19.95

Self-Employment: From Dream to Reality!
An Interactive Workbook for Starting Your Small Business
By Linda D. Gilkerson and Theresia M. Paauwe

✔ Shows readers how to conquer topics like business plans, break-even analysis, and cash flow.

✔ Contains case studies and the best activities from an 11-week training workshop designed by the authors.

Entrepreneurship • Softcover • © 1997, 8.5 x 11, 140 pp. • 1-56370-443-9 • $16.95

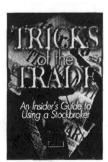

Tricks of the Trade
An Insider's Guide to Using a Stockbroker
By Mark Dempsey

✔ Looks behind the scenes—with the insight of an experienced Wall Street broker.

✔ Cites real-life examples and case studies.

✔ Uncovers investment pitfalls and offers tips for success.

Business/Personal Finance • Softcover • © 1998, 6 x 9, 243 pp. • 1-57112-084-X • $14.95

JIST Publishing · 8902 Otis Avenue · Indianapolis, IN 46216
Toll-free Ordering 1-800-648-5478